Lecture Notes in Artificial Intelligence (LNAI)

Lecture Notes in Artificial Intelligence

Subseries of Lecture Notes in Computer Science
Edited by J. Siekmann

Lecture Notes in Computer Science

Edited by G. Goos and J. Hartmanis

Editorial

Artificial Intelligence has become a major discipline under the roof of Computer Science. This is also reflected by a growing number of titles devoted to this fast developing field to be published in our Lecture Notes in Computer Science. To make these volumes immediately visible we have decided to distinguish them by a special cover as Lecture Notes in Artificial Intelligence, constituting a subseries of the Lecture Notes in Computer Science. This subseries is edited by an Editorial Board of experts from all areas of AI, chaired by Jörg Siekmann, who are looking forward to consider further AI monographs and proceedings of high scientific quality for publication.

We hope that the constitution of this subseries will be well accepted by the audience of the Lecture Notes in Computer Science, and we feel confident that the subseries will be recognized as an outstanding opportunity for publication by authors and editors of the AI community.

Editors and publisher

Lecture Notes in Artificial Intelligence

Edited by J. Siekmann

Subseries of Lecture Notes in Computer Science

481

Ewald Lang
Kai-Uwe Carstensen
Geoffrey Simmons

Modelling Spatial Knowledge on a Linguistic Basis

Theory – Prototype – Integration

Springer-Verlag

Berlin Heidelberg New York London
Paris Tokyo Hong Kong Barcelona

Authors

Ewald Lang
Fachbereich 4, Bergische Universität Wuppertal
Gauss-Straße 20, W-5600 Wuppertal 1, FRG
and
IBM Deutschland GmbH, Wissenschaftliches Zentrum
Institut für Wissensbasierte Systeme
Schloßstraße 70, W-7000 Stuttgart 1, FRG

Kai-Uwe Carstensen
Geoffrey Simmons
Fachbereich Informatik, Universität Hamburg
Bodenstedtstraße 16, W-2000 Hamburg 50, FRG

CR Subject Classification (1987): I.2.4, I.2.7

ISBN 3-540-53718-X Springer-Verlag Berlin Heidelberg New York
ISBN 0-387-53718-X Springer-Verlag New York Berlin Heidelberg

© Springer-Verlag Berlin Heidelberg 1991
Printed in Germany

Printing and binding: Druckhaus Beltz, Hemsbach/Bergstr.
2145/3140-543210 – Printed on acid-free paper

Preface

The book develops a theory about knowledge of spatial objects, which is significant for cognitive linguistics and artificial intelligence, into a new approach to knowledge structure. The theory is put into practice by means of 'rapid prototyping', in which the Prolog system "OSKAR" plays a linking role.

The book offers a two-level approach to semantic interpretation and proves that it works by means of a precise computer implementation, which in turn is applied to support a task-independent knowledge representation system. Each of these steps is described in detail, while the links are made explicit, thus retracing the evolution from theory to practice.

Following a brief Introduction, Chapter 2 outlines the three major components of the linguistic theory on which the implementation is based. Chapter 3 then gives a detailed overview of OSKAR's design and capacity. The descriptive and procedural components of the Prolog program are presented in the logical and chronological order of stages in which they have been implemented. Chapter 4 sketches the program's integration into the natural language comprehension system of the LILOG project.

The study documents interdisciplinary research at work: the model of spatial knowledge it offers is the fruit of the joint efforts of a linguist, a computational linguist and a knowledge engineer. We hope that the present work, which gives an objective report of this experience, will convince other researchers in the field of cognitive sciences that co-operation really pays off.

January 1991   Ewald Lang
                                                Kai-Uwe Carstensen
                                                Geoffrey Simmons

Contents

Der Hauswirt sagt:
Is ja' n bisken *eng*, der Hof,
aber *dafür schön hoch.*
HEINRICH ZILLE
über Berliner Hinterhöfe

The landlord says:
The courtyard may be a bit *narrow*,
but it's *nice and high.*
HEINRICH ZILLE
on Berlin backyards

* * *

A *hill* <u>can't</u> be a *valley*, you know.
That would be nonsense.
LEWIS CARROLL
Alice in Wonderland

* * *

Tiefe geht auf den *Grund*
Depth gets us to the bottom
Kai-Uwe

* * *

```
interpretation_of_DAPs_and_OS(_,
  output('No more solutions'))
              :- !
```

OSKAR

1. Introduction

1.1 Space Appeal

During the past decades, much work in the cognitive sciences has focussed on spatial issues, and today we observe a variety of projects that certainly increase, but so far do not join, their efforts towards gaining a deeper understanding of spatial knowledge. The intensity of current research as well as the diversity of approaches in this field are by no means accidental but emerge from the particular nature of spatial knowledge. What's up with spatial knowledge?

Put in a nutshell it is this:

The ubiquitity of space in our physical life-sphere and its fundamental impact on our practical behaviour are mirrored by the fundamental role of spatial knowledge and its ubiquitous impact on our cognitive behaviour. Of all discernible commonsense domains, that of spatial knowledge has the most direct but also the most complex anchoring in the perceptual apparatus of our biological endowment. Hence the diversity of approaches (psychological, linguistic, AI-oriented etc.) and the many different ways in which spatial knowledge is accessed (say, by experimenting, by constructing formal theories or by implementing systems of knowledge representation).

The present approach to the structure and processing of spatial knowledge has a share in linguistic theorizing, logic programming, and knowledge engineering, though not by lumping them together in a catch-all attempt, but by making use of them in the course of three successive steps.

The approach we are advocating takes language as a keyhole to our underlying spatial knowledge. Hence, it started with linguistic theory, i.e. by examining and adopting a certain linguistic analysis and formal account of a relevant subset of spatial expressions, namely **dimensional terms**. The next step consisted in implementing the insights thus gained in a Prolog system, thereby creating a prototype (**OSKAR**)[1] that served to prove and improve the results of the linguistic analysis. The third step (currently in progress) will embody the integration of the pertinent module into a

---

1   OSKAR is the acronym of Objekt-Schemata zur Konzeptuellen Analyse Räumlicher Objekteigenschaften (Object schemata for the conceptual analysis of spatial properties of objects).

comprehensive knowledge representation system (the **LEU/2** of **LILOG**)[2].

In short, what is novel and, we hope, promising with this approach to knowledge structure is the logical and chronological order of this three-step process:

- adoption of a **linguistic theory**
- implementation by rapid **prototyping**
- **integration** into a large knowledge representation system.

The chapters of the book, in presenting our approach to spatial knowledge, are meant to recapitulate these stages. In this way, we address ourselves to readers from different fields of cognitive science: cognitive psychologists, linguists, computational linguists, and AI-researchers.

1.2   The Context

In order to locate the present study in the context of current research on spatial cognition, it might be useful to mark out at least some of the projects which have influenced the development of the approach presented here - either by forming part of what we would accept as common framework or by advocating views which we do not share but would prefer to formulate alternatives to.

1.2.1   Linguistic Approaches

Among those current research projects which in one way or other attempt to find out *How language structures space* , the closest to ours, as regards scope and - to some extent - theoretical framework, are the projects "The spatial lexicon of French" (University of Constance) and "Spatial Localization" (University of Düsseldorf). The two-level approach to semantic interpretation (see Chap. 2) was originally developed in a comprehensive analysis of dimensional expressions (see Bierwisch/Lang 1987, 1989; Lang 1988, 1989 a, b) and, in the meantime, adopted and modified by researchers in those projects in a series of studies on

---

2   LILOG is the acronym for 'LInguistic and LOGical methods in the comprehension of German texts'. LEU/2, the second prototype of the LILOG system, was demonstrated in July of 1990.

prepositions (Schwarze 1989, Herweg 1989; Wunderlich/Herweg 1990; Kaufmann 1989, Habel 1989), verbs of position (Maienborn 1990) to name but a few. In relation to these, the present work may be considered as a contribution toward formalization and systematization. The same holds with respect to the experimental research in the acquisition and comprehension of spatial expressions within the project "Spatial Reference" (Max Planck Institute for Psycholinguistics, Nimway).

There is, of course, also much work on the semantics of spatial expressions which, though not incompatible, is at variance with our approach. A case in point is e.g. Jackendoff's (1983, 1990) claim that conceptual structure is (a subset of) semantic structure. In contrast, the two-level approach we are advocating draws heavily on keeping these two things distinct in notion as well as representation (see Chap 2 below; Bierwisch/Lang 1987, 1989; Maienborn 1990). So our claims compete with Jackendoff's claims in some relevant respects, thus sharpening the discussion of the basics.

Finally, there are linguistic approaches to spatial knowledge which we would basically disagree with. For instance, the conclusions of a recent monograph on "Language and Spatial Cognition" start with the complaint: "Attempts to give an account of lexical meaning remain the weakest link in artificial intelligence and logical semantics. Neither discipline has ever offered lexical representations that satisfactorily account for speakers' uses; both have discovered that lexical meanings simply cannot be regimented into neat bundles of necessary and sufficient conditions."(Herskovits 1986:193)

While one may fully agree with the first part of this statement as concerns the actual state of the art, one may be less pessimistic about the claim that lexical meanings are resistant to a clear-cut analysis on principled grounds. The two-level approach to the semantics of spatial expressions we propose in Chap. 2 differs markedly from the approach taken by Herskovits (or by related work within a prototype-semantics framework e.g. Vandeloise 1986, Langacker 1986, Hottenroth 1988, Lakoff 1987, 1988). It will suffice to mark some of the major points of divergence by key-words.

Modularity.   While other approaches are implicit in this respect, the two-level approach explicitly ascribes to the view that our cognitive behaviour is essentially based on structures and processes which are determined by the interaction of relatively autonomous systems and subsystems called 'modules'. This is the basic assumption which the two-level approach attempts to elaborate in tackling crucial problems of lexical semantics like the following:

(a) How to interrelate the lexical meanings of spatial terms with the morpho-syntactic category features assigned to them ?

(b) How to draw a justified distinction between the linguistically coded semantic contents of a lexical item and the range of contextual specifications it may undergo ?

(c) How to distinguish between, but at the same time allow for the interaction of, word meanings as part of linguistic knowledge and concepts as part of everyday or world knowledge ?

Evidently, these questions are aimed at specifying appropriate interfaces between different levels of mental representation, and it is along these lines that the two-level approach has suggestions to give and solutions to offer.

Conceptual basis.   As regards the source of spatial knowledge and the inventory of conceptual elements that are made use of in the descriptive framework, the 'experiential' approach adopted by Herskovits and others is, roughly speaking, **observer-centered** and **situation-based**. That is, the primary concepts for approaching the meaning of locative expressions are defined in terms of prototypical **situation types** which involve a human being in "canonical position" (standing upright on horizontal ground) as the central source for orientational cues.

In contrast, the two-level approach we subscribe to may be called **object-centered** and **axes-based**, as it primarily draws on an inventory of categorized **object concepts** and the categorization grids defining their constitutive spatial properties. In this approach, spatial knowledge is basically organized by what we call the **Primary Perceptual Space**, that is, a system of axes that define our internal model of external space. Though it is difficult to compare the ontologies of both approaches, we dare say the latter is more general and comprehensive, as it seems to obey Occams razor more clearly than Herskovits' system, for example.

Formalization   The modular approach forwarded here also entails a different attitude toward the role of formalization in linguistic theorizing. While Herskovits, with reference to "the subtlety and complexity of language use" (1986:19), does not see any advantage in formal representation or implementation, we take the stand that implementing a (sufficiently formalized) linguistic analysis may prove to be a very useful means to check up the consistency and exhaustiveness of the underlying theory (see Chap. 3 below).

Concerning the "imagery debate" on propositional vs. depictorial representation of spatial knowledge, our approach, as it starts from linguistic structure, is a contribution to the former. It should be noted, however, that the information available in our representational format for object concepts (see Section 2.3) is basically that which the creation of "mental images" of objects invokes (for details of depictorial and analogue representations see Kosslyn 1980, Habel 1988, 1990, Rehkämper 1988). Furthermore, as will become clear from Sections 2.1 and 2.2, this kind of information is also fully compatible with the object-centered represent-ations postulated by Marr (1982) and at least in some respects with the viewer-centered representations postulated by others (cf. Pinker 1984 for an overview and, e.g., Farah 1988 for the relationship between imagery and perception).

1.2.2 Implementations

There are a number of implemented fragments of the domain of spatial concepts on the market. Among these we should mention the "Languages of Spatial Relations Initiative" of the National Center for Geographic Information and Analysis (SUNY, Buffalo, NY), which mainly endeavours to capture large-scale space for applicational purposes. In comparison, our objective is a fine-grained account of object properties of small-scale space. Fragments of related areas (prepositions, verbs of motion, and nouns denoting designated object parts in French) have been implemented within the project "The semantics of spatial expressions" (Toulouse University). An alternative implementation of the dimensional adjective analysis of Bierwisch/Lang (1987), applied to English data and within a different framework, has been presented by Wenger (1988).

1.2.3 The LILOG-Project

One undertaking in which a considerable amount of research activity in computational linguistics has taken place since 1986 is the project LILOG at IBM Germany. LILOG´s objective is to develop a text comprehension system that extracts knowledge from texts resulting in representations used to answer questions about those texts in a natural language dialogue. Since space and time constitute inevitable ingredients of any situation, a system aspiring to "comprehension of natural-language texts" has to cope with a broad spectrum of linguistic material related to them.[3]

A major part of the work presented in this study was done at the University of Hamburg in connection with the subproject LILOG-R (R for "Raum" [Space]). In Hamburg, a unified representational format is being developed that is capable of linking propositional with depictional representations of spatial knowledge. This strategy encompasses the structural analysis of linguistic expressions of motion and localization (typical of route descriptions, tourist guides, etc.), which primarily draw on topological relations in large-scale space environments. This is where the present work enters the picture by complementing topology with geometry, thereby reflecting the fact that spatial knowledge is organized by the interaction of topological (localizations of and distances between objects in large-scale space) and geometric principles (axes and positions of objects in small-scale space).

In 1988, there was no simple way of integrating the semantic theory of Lang (1987) into the LILOG system. First, the theory had not yet been tested for consistency and completeness so that it would have been too early to integrate it at all. Second, the structures described by the theory were underspecified with respect to algorithms operating on them. Third, at the time the integration was envisaged, most of the components of the LILOG system needed for representing and processing knowledge had not yet been fully developed. Moreover, the global knowledge structures now available in the LILOG system were still on the drawing board then. In view of all this, it seemed best to establish an independent prototype as an intermediate stage: that was the birth of OSKAR.

The Prolog program OSKAR presented in Chap. 3 has not only contributed to a deeper understanding of *How language structures space*, but has also clarified the ontology and architecture needed for modelling spatial knowledge in a large comprehension system. The integration of

---

3   See Herzog et al. (1986) for a detailed statement of the goals of the LILOG project. Bosch et al. (1991) contains a collection of papers documenting the various components of the system, including Carstensen/Simmons (1991), which Chap. 4 is based on (see also Geurts (1990) for an intermediate report on the project).

OSKAR´s representations and procedures into LEU/2 of the LILOG system is elaborated in Chap. 4.

1.3   The Issue: What Constitutes Spatial Knowledge?

Regarding the determinants of spatial knowledge, the much-discussed question of whether space defines objects, i.e., space is conceived as a container within which objects can be located, positioned, and interrelated (=Container View), or whether objects define space, i.e., space is made up of relations between objects (=Configuration View), should best be answered with: both views are applicable! Actually, spatial knowledge can be shown to draw on both ways of conceiving space. It comprises both conceptual knowledge of objects as entities to be identified by their spatial properties and an (internal) mental model of (external) physical space which determines the way in which objects are conceived of as being positioned and located in space. To put it briefly and concisely:

(A) Knowledge of an object embodies knowledge of the object's spatial dimensions, that is, of the gradable characteristics of its typical, possible or actual, extension in space.
(B) Knowledge of space implies the availability of some system of axes which determine the designation of certain dimensions of, and distances between, objects in space.

Thus, spatial knowledge covers the area in which object knowledge and orientation ability intersect and interact. Within the realms of cognition, spatial knowledge constitutes a fundamental modularly structured system which organizes the representation and processing of perceptually based and conceptually categorized information. The description and modelling of a major module of this system forms the very content of this report.

For the goals of AI research, the task to model the structure and processing of spatial knowledge is as crucial as it is complicated ; *crucial* - due to the importance of space to the cognitive system as a whole: the structure of spatial knowledge forms the basic pattern which is transferred to other conceptual domains (time, acoustics, social hierarchy, etc.), and *complicated* - due to the empirical inaccessibility of the concepts to be modeled. Spatial knowledge is ubiquitous and is bound up with all cognitive processes so intimately that special techniques are required to elicit the specific features of this system of knowledge. Any attempt to model spatial knowledge within an AI framework would thus be well-advised to seriously cultivate cooperation and communication with adjacent sciences, not least with linguistic semantics and cognitive psychology.

1.4   A First Glance at OSKAR's Capabilities

In this book, we will propose a new approach to modeling an important subset of spatial knowledge by presenting the Prolog program OSKAR. The relevant pieces of knowledge have been accessed in several subsequent steps, starting from a fine-grained analysis of spatial expressions in natural language and ending up with a conceptual model of how physical objects are conceived as spatial entities along the lines of (A) and (B) above. The range of knowledge which the program is designed to cope with comprises several separable but intricately related domains of spatial cognition. To put it in a nutshell, OSKAR is capable of accounting for

(1) **Dimensional designation of objects** - by specifying a (presumably exhaustive) set of rules and principles according to which physical objects are assigned spatial dimensions such as length, width, height, depth, thickness etc.

As a prerequisite for setting up the rules of (1) and likewise as a result of checking their applicability, objects have to be classified appropriately. Therefore, OSKAR also provides for

(2) **Categorization of spatial objects** - by a (supposedly universal) taxonomy which categorizes objects as to their dimensionable gestalt and position properties and correlates the latter with the objects' movability.

Moreover, as a result of exploiting (1) and (2) in order to spell out the full range of positional variants a given object may assume, OSKAR has been elaborated further to master

(3) **Positional specification of objects** - by means of procedures for evaluating the possible or actual spatial positions of a given object (as lying down, standing upright / upside down / edgewise, being turned to the right, tipped over etc.)

Now, the claim that OSKAR is designed to simulate the structure and processing of a certain subset of spatial knowledge can be made in two respects. In the first place, it is no doubt very useful to have an implemented system that answers all sorts of queries concerning (1) - (3) by providing *all and nothing but the correct solutions* as output. In this sense, the program certainly simulates crucial aspects of cognitive behaviour: (a) it reveals to a large extent how language structures space, and by that means (b) it tells us quite a lot about how we conceptualize the spatial environment we live in. This assessment holds independent of the particular set-up of the program at issue.

But there is still another respect in which OSKAR deserves interest, namely, the way it took *from* the first attempt to implement a fully worked out linguistic analysis *via* various modifications *up to* the (tentatively) final shape it has got now. Of course, it is not the usual tinkering-with and patching-up of programs which is worth mentioning. However, notice should be taken of the remarkable feed-back between object theory and program that happened to emerge in the course of implementation. This feedback had its effects on three distinct levels from which the theory - program relationship can be viewed.

First.   Re-writing a set of (sufficiently formalized) linguistic rules and principles in Prolog has certainly proved to be a highly useful means to check up the consistency and exhaustiveness of the linguistic theorizing that produced them. In this respect, OSKAR has lead to a couple of minor corrections that appeared necessary to secure the theory's observational adequacy.

Second.   In the process of working out the details of dimensional designation in Prolog, our view on the basic cognitive devices involved was remarkably sharpened - with the effect of enabling us to discover, and in consequence to incorporate in OSKAR, the intimate relationship between (1) and (3). The connection between dimensioning and positioning an object is determined by a set of intertwined conditions based on which some object x gets assigned its proper dimensions, its intrinsic and/or deictic sides, and the range of its possible positional variants. In short, implementing a theory can turn into supplementing it.

Third.   There is, in addition, a more philosophical issue which ought to be mentioned. The present authors fully ascribe to the view that one has to be extremely cautious <u>not</u> to make the mistake of ascribing (whatever sort of) "psychological reality" to formal models of linguistic or factual knowledge, no matter whether they are available in terms of linguistics proper or in terms of Prolog programming. There should be no doubt about that. In view of David Marr's (1982) celebrated three-level distinction for information-processing devices, however, specifically as regards the relationship between the Computational theory level and the level of Representation and algorithms, it may perhaps be of interest to draw a comparison between theory and program on the level of their respective modularity. Thus it seems to be rewarding to look for any non-arbitrary correspondences between the modular structure of the theory to be implemented and the various building blocks of the program implementing it. In this respect, OSKAR might provide a case in point. We shall not delve into this problem, however, but leave it at that.

1.5   How the Book is Organized

In order to keep what was advertised above, the presentation mirrors the chronological and logical order of the development stages (I) to (III), which, when arranged to sections, will result in the following layout:

(I)   Approaching spatial knowledge by analyzing the semantics of natural language object names and dimensional expressions within a two-level model (as proposed in Bierwisch/Lang 1987, 1989; Lang 1987, 1988, 1989 a, b), which forms the general framework - **Section 2.1**

Defining Dimension Assignment Parameters (DAPs) and setting up Object Schemata (OS) as a representational means to model the relevant features of object concepts, and formulating rules which, in terms of object schemata, construe the semantic interpretation of dimensional expressions as processing operations on representations of spatial knowlege - **Sections 2.2 - 2.5**

(II)   Implementing dimensional designation and positional variation of spatial objects in the Prolog program OSKAR - **Chapter 3**

(III)   Integrating OSKAR into the representational formalism of the second version of the LILOG system (LEU/2) - **Chapter 4**

In this paper, we use the following **typographic conventions:**

text font / style	used to indicate
italics	linguistic expressions under analysis
CAPS	meaning components of linguistic expressions
"...."	conceptual representations (concepts)
SMALL CAPS	theoretically relevant notions
<u>underline</u>	emphasis
bold face	emphasis
courier	Prolog code/L$_{LILOG}$ code

1.6 Acknowledgements

This book is a reworked and extended version of an IBM IWBS Report (Lang/Carstensen 1990). Its preparation was partially supported by a guest scientist grant of IBM Germany to Ewald Lang. We are grateful to Jörg Siekmann for including this volume in the *Lecture Notes in Artificial Intelligence* Series. The two non-native-speaking authors wish to express their gratitude to the native-speaking co-author for polishing up their English: thank you, Geoff.

2. A Linguistic Approach to Spatial Knowledge

2.0 Introductory Remarks

The linguistic theory which forms the background of the present approach has been developed as an attempt to trace mental representations from the level of sensory input conditions through conceptual structure to their lexical and grammatical organization. That is, language has served as a key hole to take a look into otherwise barely accessible levels of mental structure formation. This will suffice to say that it is too complex to be presented here in detail. We cannot even broadly outline that part of the theory which specifically deals with dimensional designation. On the other hand, we have to provide the gentle reader with that minimum of background information that will enable her/him to follow the line of argumentation and, we hope, to get a taste of how much sophistication is needed to obtain efficient models of spatial knowledge.

Thus, in the following we will confine ourselves to sketch the basic assumptions and main tenets of the theory while introducing some of its basic concepts and illustrating them with a couple of well-tried examples and with the help of illustrative diagrams. With regard to anything else, the reader is referred to the series of studies in Bierwisch/Lang (1987, 1989); Lang (1987, 1988, 1989 a, b).

2.1 Dimensional Designation: General Framework

2.1.1 Basic Assumptions on Mental Structures

The general investigational framework is determined by the following list of interlinked assumptions, which are labelled with • key-words to enable quick reference and to facilitate comprehension:

• **Modularity.** Basically, all human cognitive behavior is organized in a modular fashion. The structure formation underlying any concrete behavioral performance is based upon the integration of various relatively autonomous, task-specifically interacting systems and subsystems (MODULES). Language, the different modes of perception, and the conceptual organisation of experience make up such systems, which for their part are again structured in a modular way. The aim to be derived from this assumption is to identify the different systems, to analize their structure and organisation in the attempt to capture the rationale behind their interaction.

• **Representations**: ELEMENTS, RULES and PRINCIPLES. Each of the individual structure-forming systems and subsystems comprises a distinct inventory of categorized ELEMENTS that are configurated to more complex representations SR, according to appropriate RULES which, in turn, are determined as to their format by both system-specific and general PRINCIPLES.

• **Autonomy** and **Interaction**. A system S is autonomous to the extent that the representations SR, determined by S, are determined by specific principles which are only valid for S.

Two systems S_1 and S_2 interact to the extent that the representations SR_i, determined by S_i, contain parameters which are instantiated by appropriate values from the representations SR_j, determined by S_j.

• **Structure** vs. **Processing**. The representations SR, determined by a system S, represent the structural aspect of certain mental states in the interaction between organism and environment, i.e. the STRUCTURE OF IMPLICIT KNOWLEDGE (mainly beyond the control of the conscious mind) which is constituted by the system S. The processual aspect of the system S comprises the mental processes which arise in phylogenesis, ontogenesis, and task-oriented immediate generation of representations, that is, processes by which SR can be produced, restructured, and related to external conditions and stimuli.

The structure of a cognitive system S is the result of ontogenetic developments which are determined by two factors:

(a)   by the underlying internal preconditions of the organism;
(b)   by the experiences assimilated on the basis of these preconditions.

The internal preconditions form the structure of an initial state which is modified and specified, depending on the acquisitive nature of the particular system, until a relatively stable final state, characterized by the system S assumed above, is reached. The structure of the initial state forms the basis and the framework, within which the systems of knowledge to be acquired can vary. The structure of the initial state thus organizes the assimilation of the input and therefore the construction of the resulting system of knowledge. This framework is determined by a system of principles and parameters whose organismic basis is the result of phylogenetic processes.

Fig.1 provides a schema of these interrelations. The principles will be taken up in sections 2.2 - 2.4 below. The dotted window marks that subset which we will focus on next.

Fig. 1   Structural and Processual Aspects of Knowledge

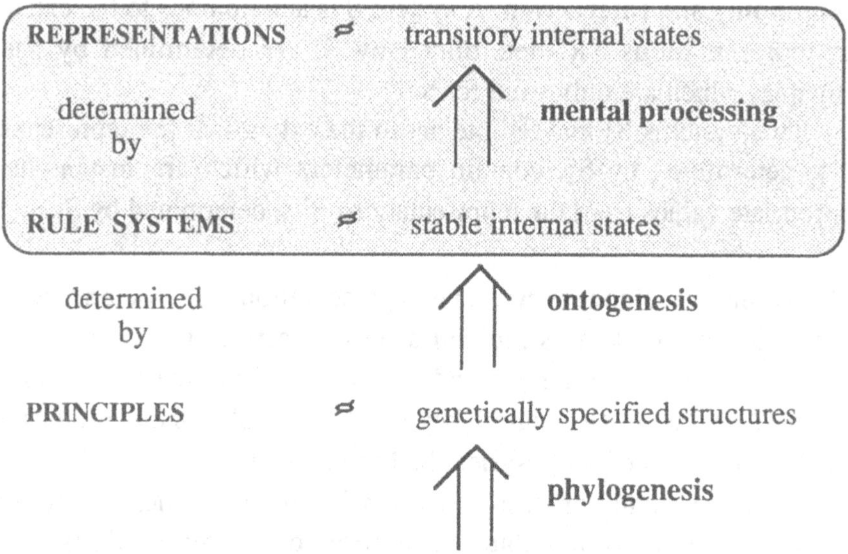

2.1.2   Language and Cognition

Of the cognitive systems involved in the different concrete forms of linguistic behaviour, mainly two, each based upon independent principles, are to be looked at here: the language system whose structure of knowledge consists of the grammar **G**, and the conceptual system, for which a structured system of knowledge **C** is to be assumed. In general, for every linguistic expression LE as determined by **G** there is an interpretation in **C**, but not every conceptual structure is the interpretation of a linguistic expression. Specifically, the following assumptions are made:

(5)   THE STRUCTURE OF **G**

(5.1)   A system of principles and parameters **UG** (=Universal Grammar) determines the framework of possible grammars **G**, i.e. grammars which can be acquired under normal conditions.

(5.2)   A grammar **G** is a complex system of rules and conditions determining a class of internal structural representations SR.

(5.3)   A structural representation SR defines the internal state which underlies the production and/or comprehension of a linguistic utterance LU, i.e. a linguistic expression LE interpreted in a context CT, and thus characterizes the features of the expression LE as determined by the linguistic knowledge **G**.

(5.4)   The SR, determined by **G**, represent the linguistic knowledge underlying a linguistic expression LE as an integrated result of several relatively autonomous but interacting modules of structure formation.

(6)   THE STRUCTURE OF **C**

(6.1)   Form and substance of the internal representations determined by the conceptual system **C** are poorly understood as yet. It is assumed, however, that **C** (in analogy to **G**) emerges ontogenetically from a universal schema **UC** which comprises the species-specific principles of conceptualization. Besides this, two substantial claims are made:

(6.2)   The representations determined by **C** provide access to conceptualized experience as organized in various cognitive subsystems, among them the visual, auditory, motor, motivational, and, of course, the linguistic system, which for the purposes of the present study serves as probe and peephole.

(6.3)   The system of conceptual knowledge **C** has to be construed as the representational mediator with respect to the interaction of the various cognitive subsystems. In view of its INTERMODAL ACCESSIBILITY, **C** is taken to determine a unified level of structural representation CS to which the autonomous representations of the various subsystems of **C** can be related and hence interrelated among each other.

(6.4) Within C we will provisionally delimit some subsystem C_{SPACE}. which relates the structure of physical space to mental representations. Thus, C_{SPACE} is construed as that conceptual module which determines the way in which spatial information, no matter whether sensory-inputted or linguistically encoded, is processed. The semantic analysis of dimensional adjectives may thus serve as a window to look at the internal structure of C_{SPACE}.

(7)   THE INTERACTION OF G AND C

(7.1) The BASIC ELEMENTS OF C, here conceived of as conceptual features, combine into more complex configurations which represent concepts. Relations between C and G are established when concepts are assigned syntactically categorized phonological labels to form stable memorized lexical items, i.e. the so-called MENTAL LEXICON.

(7.2) For any simple or complex linguistic expression LE, the grammar G determines a set of interlinked representations SR(LE) which specify the **phon**ological, **morph**ological, **synt**actic, and **sem**antic structure of LE. The phonological structure is interpreted by articulatory and perceptual patterns, whereas the semantic structure of LE is mapped onto representations of CONCEPTUAL STRUCTURE. Fig.2 below, which exemplifies the area marked in Fig.1 with regard to linguistic and conceptual knowledge, provides a rough picture of the relations and components involved. Again, the dotted window indicates the area we will turn to next.

(7.3) As indicated by the overlap in Fig. 2, it is the internal semantic structure of lexical items that serves as an interface between C and G (that is, between conceptual knowledge and linguistic knowledge), and it is the specification of the interfacial properties of syntactically combined lexical items that forms the very heart of the linguistic approach to spatial knowledge presented here. We will take a closer look at this interface in section 2.1.5 below.

Fig. 2   Interaction of Linguistic and Conceptual Knowledge

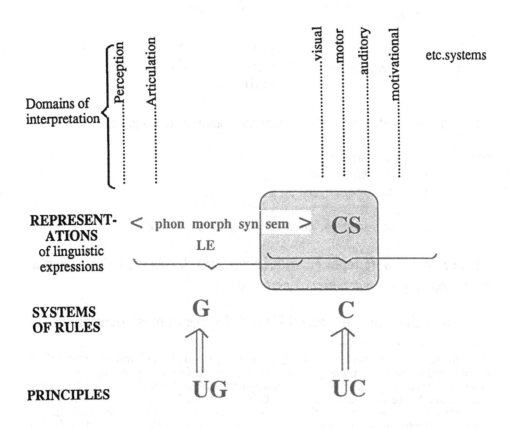

2.1.3   Dimensional Designation: The Scope of Data

The starting point was a detailed semantic analysis of the distribution and interpretation conditions of German spatial dimensional adjectives (DAdj) including:

(8)   (a)   *lang - kurz*   *breit - schmal*   *dick - dünn*

long - short   { wide broad } - narrow   thick - thin

(b)   *hoch - niedrig*   *tief - flach*
high - low   deep - shallow

(c)   *weit - eng*   *weit - nah*

$\left\{\begin{array}{l}\text{wide}\\ \text{broad}\end{array}\right\}$ - narrow   far - near

(d)   *groß - klein* $\left\{\begin{array}{l}\text{big} - \text{little}\\ \text{large} - \text{small}\\ \text{tall} - \text{short}\end{array}\right\}$4

occurring in a wide range of grammatical constructions such as

(9)   x   ist   3m *lang*
        x   ist   *kürzer* als   y,
        x   ist   *größer* als   y,
        x   ist   so *breit* wie   y,
        x   ist   weniger *hoch, tief, eng* als   y   etc.

where x and y were replaced with names for (classes of) objects such as
board, pole, tower, gate, tunnel, plate, book etc..

Through empirical research[5], the full range of restrictions on the co-

---

4   In order to save space, we will (a) not add glosses to every German example cited;
(b) stick to English in the running text where linguistic differences are negligible.
 The more serious question: What is language-specific and what is universal with this
analysis and hence with the scope of data OSKAR is suited to handle? will be discussed
in section 2.5. -   As a rule of thumb it holds that semantically English and German
dimensional adjectives are very similar (excepting the differences marked by {...} in
(8)), but there are more distinctions to be observed regarding the meaning equivalence of
object names between the two languages.

5   Besides making extensive use of the author's linguistic intuition the data were
collected by means of various **tests**, including (a) **Object guessing** - Subjects were
presented with sentences like those listed in the left part of (i) and asked to replace x by
an appropriate name of a spatial object.

(i)   x is *long, wide, and high*   (x = *table, chest, brick,...*)
             x is *wide, deep, and high*   (x = *board,tunnel,chest,...*)
*   x is *wide, thick, and deep*   (no value for x found)
*   x is *deep and thick*   (no value for x found)
             x is *high/tall and thick*   (x = *tower, tree, pole*) etc.

(b) **Naming object extents** - Subjects were given pictures showing simple geometric
figures that were claimed to represent concrete spatial objects, say, a brick or a
tombstone, and the subjects had to name the extensions by DAdjs as in (ii):

(ii)   *The brick is 24cm* $\left\{\begin{array}{l}\text{long}\\ \text{high}\\ \text{wide}\\ \text{deep}\\ \text{*thick}\end{array}\right\}$ *, 11cm* $\left\{\begin{array}{l}\text{wide}\\ \text{high}\\ \text{deep}\\ \text{*long}\\ \text{*thick}\end{array}\right\}$ *, and 7cm* $\left\{\begin{array}{l}\text{thick}\\ \text{high}\\ \text{wide}\\ \text{*long}\end{array}\right\}$

occurrence of DAdjs (e.g. no object can be *tall, deep and thick* simultaneously) as well as on the combination of DAdjs with object names (a garden cannot be *tall* ; a tunnel can be either *high, wide and long* or *high, wide and deep* etc.) was specified. To give an idea of the combinatorics involved, we quote a couple of observational statements on the structure of the data base. We add brief comments on how these observations were arranged in search for principles that would explain the facts.

(10)   Drawing on the six German DAdjs *lang, hoch, breit, weit, tief, dick* (all of (8) except *groß*), it holds that:

Out of	20	possible	3 term	combinations there are only	10,
	15		2 term		9,
	6		1 term		1,

which are/is interpretable as a suitable description of the dimensions of some object *x*.

These combinatorial restrictions are indicative of the DIMENSIONALITY (1D, 2D, or 3D) of the object to which a DAdj may be applied. This has lead to the formulation of conditions like (11):

(11)   *lang*   may be applied to a   1D, 2D, or 3D object
        hoch, breit   require a   2D or 3D object
        dick, weit, tief require a   3D object

Moreover, constraints like those in (11) lead to COMPATIBILITY CONDITIONS within a DAdj-combination to be applied to some object *x*. Among them :

(12)   *dick, tief*   never combine with respect to the same object *x*
        lang, dick   never designate the same object extent
        breit, weit   can alternatively designate the same object extent
                        etc.

(c) **Positioning objects.** In an acting-out task, subjects were given an identified object of fixed size, say, a book or a brick, and they were asked to position the object according to its possible description by sentences like those in (i) or (ii). For details, see Lang 1988, 1989.

In addition to (11) and (12), there are RESTRICTIONS ON VARIATION :

(13)   Within the 20 interpretable combinations of DAdjs as listed in (10),
        which arithmetically yield 78 possible variations, there are only 40
        interpretable ones.

RESTRICTIONS ON VARIATION indicate crucial aspects of OBJECT CATE-
GORIZATION. Thus, among other things, dimensionally designated objects
are categorized as to their ORIENTATION and/or PERSPECTIVIZATION, that
is, as to the object's reference to the surrounding space. Take just two sets
of examples illustrating a variety of ways in which dimensional designation
relates to an object's reference to its surroundings.

(14)   The distribution of *hoch* subdivides 3D objects into four subclasses
        of objects with respect to having

                (a) fixed orientation   (mountain, river)
                (b) canonical orientation   (tower, desk)
                (c) inherent orientation   (book, picture)
        or   (d) being unspecified as to orientation   (brick, pole)

(15)   The distribution of *tief* subdivides 3D objects into three subclasses
        of objects with respect to having

                (a) canonical perspectivization   (river, ditch)
                (b) inherent perspectivization   (hole, wound)
        or   (c) being unspecified as to perspective   (brick, board)

We will return to ORIENTATION and/or PERSPECTIVIZATION of objects in
section 2.2.3, and to OBJECT CATEGORIZATION in section 2.5 below.

        To sum up, the scope of linguistic data based on which a theory of
dimensional designation has to be devised includes two overlapping sets of
facts to be explained. These include (a) the total of possible, that is,
regularly interpretable, combinations of DAdjs with object names, (b) the
range of interpretations each particular combination of DAdjs with an
object name may be assigned to. Note the wide range of interpretations
which e.g. *The brick is wide enough but not high enough* may have as to the

brick's position in relation to the surrounding space. It takes more than a moment's reflection to realize that there are at least 6 possibilities!

2.1.4 Preview of the Theory

Having outlined the complexity of the data to be accounted for, it may be useful to take an overview of the theory by briefly tracing the steps of its development.

The facts reported in section 2.1.3 above gave rise to the understanding that dimensional expressions[6] refer to certain axis-determined GESTALT and/or POSITION PROPERTIES of objects, and thereby designate them as spatial dimensions of the objects at issue. So *lang-kurz* [*long-short*] always refer to an object's maximal axis, *hoch-niedrig* [*high-low, tall-short*] to a vertically oriented axis, *dick-dünn* [*thick-thin*] to a substance-determined axis, *tief* [*deep*] to an observer-defined axis, etc.

Semantically, the dimensional expressions are thus to be taken to represent (among other things) linguistic parameters for designating pertinent object axes. They are henceforth called DIMENSION ASSIGNMENT PARAMETERS (DAPs) and given mnemotechnic abbreviations like MAX, VERT, OBS etc.. We will discuss them in more detail in section 2.2.2 below.

The semantic representation of object names (*board, tower, water* etc.) contains appropriate information on the object's boundedness (to sort out objects from substances), its one-, two-, or three-dimensionality, and its salient axial properties. For e.g. *Stange* [*pole*], it states that a pole is a bounded, three-dimensional object with a maximal axis (identifiable by the parameter MAX contained in *lang-kurz*) and with two integrated axes (identifiable by the parameter SUB contained in *dick-dünn* [*thick-thin*]). The meaning of the word *Stange* comprises only the linguistically encoded address for access to the concept "pole", that is, to a categorized element of our general knowledge of objects which is fixed in long-term memory.

---

6   Although the studies under review focus on dimensional expressions of category Adjective - cf. (8) - (15) above, one should keep in mind that the principles that control dimensional designation are equally involved in a wide variety of related expressions of different categories, among them Nouns (*length, longitude, height, altitude, tallness; highway, long jump, short wave,...*); Verbs (*widen, lengthen, shorten*); Adverbs (*fly low,* sink *deep,* butter *thickly, ...*); Prepositions (*along, below, over, in front of*), and an enormous number of phrases (*in depth, put in lengthwise, etc.*). That's why we feel entitled to speak of dimensional expressions in general.

Under this view it follows that the concept "pole" is language-independent in that it is equally accessible to equivalent names from different languages (say *Stange, pole, perche* etc.) or also to a non-verbal, *e.g.* visual or tactile, representation of a pole.

The theory thus draws heavily on keeping the notions "semantic" and "conceptual" distinct while at the same time providing a full account of their interaction.

2.1.5   Linguistic vs. Conceptual Level

The analysis of dimensional designation has led to the establishment of a model of semantic interpretation (as involved in language comprehension and language production alike) in which two levels of knowledge representation are differentiated from, and specifically mapped onto, each other:

(16) A level representing language-bound word meanings (= **Semantic Form** (SF - level)), at which the dimensional expressions appear as grammatically coded Dimension Assignment Parameters (DAPs) for designating object axes and the object names as addresses for access to object concepts. The Semantic Form of a lexical item constitutes an integral part of the information comprised by its entry in the lexicon. More on the LEXICAL ENTRY of DAdj will follow immediately.

(17) A level representing language-independent, intermodally accessible elements and complexes of conceptual knowledge (= **Conceptual Structure** (CS - level)), at which the object concepts appear in the form of OBJECT SCHEMATA. The latter contain entries which instantiate the Dimension Assignment Parameters (DAP) encoded in the dimension expressions. More on this in section 2.3. below.

On this approach, Semantic Form is considered to be the INTERFACE between grammatically determined linguistic knowledge and conceptually determined everyday or encyclopedic knowledge about the world, while Conceptual Structure is taken to provide a unified level of representation to which visual, auditory, motor, and, of course, linguistic information can be related and hence be interrelated among each other. We wish to outline just three arguments to justify the separation of the two levels and to illustrate their interaction.

<u>First</u>.   Without drawing a clear distinction between language-bound semantic and intermodally accessible conceptual representations, it is impossible to explain why, say, the sentence *Das Brett ist breit genug* [*the board is wide enough*], regarding the object extent which is to be identified by *breit* [*wide*], has the same range of interpretations when applied to the spatial situations shown in (18)(I-III), which form non-verbal contexts, as when embedded in the verbal contexts ... *und lang* or *und hoch* or *und tief genug, aber zu dünn* provided in (19)(1-3).

(18)   I   II   III

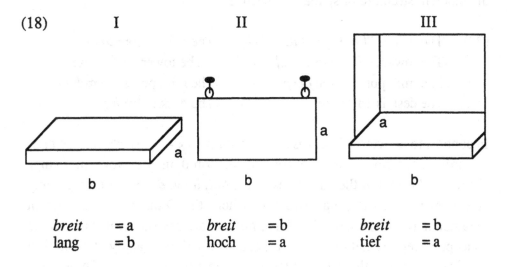

| *breit* | = a | *breit* | = b | *breit* | = b |
| *lang* | = b | *hoch* | = a | *tief* | = a |

(19)
(1) *Das Brett ist breit* und <u>lang</u> genug, aber zu dünn (*breit* = a as in I)
(2) *Das Brett ist breit* und <u>hoch</u> genug, aber zu dünn(*breit* = b as in II)
(3) *Das Brett ist breit* und <u>tief</u> genug, aber zu dünn (*breit* = b as in III)
       [*The board is wide* and <u>long/high/deep</u> *enough* but too thin]

The possible equivalence of verbal and non-verbal contexts for determining the interpretation of linguistic expressions such as *breit* [*wide*] provides strong evidence for the claim that the contextual restrictions involved must be accounted for and checked against each other at the intermodally accessible level of conceptual structure representation (CS-level).

<u>Second</u>. Without the assumption that semantic interpretation involves two levels, one is forced to treat dimensional adjectives like *breit* or object names like *Brett* as hopelessly polysemous expressions, which contradicts their actual usability and would run counter to general aspects of learnability. In the two-level semantics proposed, the obvious many-to-

many relation between dimension expressions and object extents (of which (18) and (19) give just a sample) is accounted for by the relationship between a Dimension Assignment Parameter at the level of Semantic Form and the specifically restrained range of its instantiations at the level of Conceptual Structure.

Third.   Only the two-level semantic approach provides the means to treat the following valid ($\longrightarrow$) or invalid ($\nrightarrow$) inferences correctly, that is, as relations which hold between object concepts and which thereby determine the inherent structure of spatial knowledge.

(20)   The pole is 20m *high / tall* $\longrightarrow$ The pole is 20m *long*

        The tower is 20m *high / tall* $\nrightarrow$ * The tower is 20m *long*

        The milk pot is 30cm *deep* $\longrightarrow$ The milk pot is 30cm *high*

        The desk is 1m *deep* $\nrightarrow$ The desk is 1m *high*

In contrast to converses like *x is longer than y* $\longleftrightarrow$ *y is shorter than x,* the inferences noted in (20) are not anchored in the word meanings (Semantic Forms) of the adjectives *high, tall, long, deep,* but emerge only at the level of Conceptual Structure where the Dimension Assignment Parameters (DAPs) encoded in *high, tall* etc. are assigned values from the conceptual representations of the objects to which they apply. To take just the first example: the representation of the object concepts "pole" and "tower" both contain the information that their height is their vertically oriented length. But in the case of "pole", the orientation is induced contextually such that a pole's length derives from, or is entailed by, its height; whereas in the case of "tower", the orientation is intrinsic in such a way that a tower's length is not detachable from its height. As regards models of spatial knowledge, the capability of a theory to provide an account for the inferences in (16) has become a touchstone of its adequacy.

   The distinction between SF - level and CS - level marks one of the major points in which the present approach to semantics differs from previous analyses, notably from research work treating the same or related lexical material within a semantic marker framework (cf. Bierwisch 1967; Hlebec 1983; Lafrenz 1983; Lehrer 1974; Lyons 1977) or within a prototype semantics approach (cf. Herskovits 1986, 1988). Revealing as it may be, we cannot delve into a discussion of the pros and cons of the various proposals.

The crucial point of the approach presented here is the role it attributes to the internal structure of lexical items. Returning to (16) we should like to add some brief remarks on the lexical entry of DAdjs. As an element of the lexicon of the given language, a lexical item comprises several sorts of structural information defining its relations to the other subsystems of **G**. Besides information regarding phonetic form and syntactic categorization, the entries for DAdjs contain a representation of their Semantic Form specifying the componential structure of their lexical meaning. Omitting technical details, all DAdjs meet the following schema:

(21) $[[\text{QUANT DIM } x] = [v \pm c]]$

QUANT is a semantic prime for a scaling operation which assigns a scale value composed of v and c to some spatial object x with regard to a dimension d. The latter is represented here by the placeholder DIM, a variable to be replaced by a limited set of constants (MAX, SUB, VERT, OBS, DIST...) which specify the dimensional meaning component of the items listed in (8) above.

The components 'QUANT', '=', 'v', and 'c' are needed to account for gradation; the component '$\pm$' is responsible for the polar organization of DAdjs. These components will be disregarded for the rest of the paper. OSKAR is primarily designed to cope with dimensional designation and positional variation of objects in space. Some details on the nature and interpretation of the constants replacing DIM are given in section 2.2.2 below.

Having set up the basics thus far, we may now summarize the assumptions outlined in this subsection in the diagram in Fig. 3 below, which in a way displays a magnified and more detailed view of that subset of Fig. 2 which is marked by the dotted square.

Without retelling the whole story of the semantics of dimensional designation (which is elaborated at length in Lang 1987, 1988, 1989 a, b), we will now turn to the three major components of the theory. As can be seen from Fig. 3, these are the following:

(22)   (a) the **Dimension Assignment Parameters (DAPs)**
            (cf. the element VERT in the Semantic Form of *hoch*)

      (b) the **Object Schemata (OS)**
            (cf. the object concepts x_1, x_2,...., determined by the conceptual
            submodule C_{SPACE})

      (c) the suitable **device for mapping** the former onto the latter
            (cf. the pencil of dotted lines indicating the various ways in
            which VERT refers to an object axis)

In line with the modularity assumption noted above, each of the components of the theory listed in (22) has to be justified on independent grounds, and all of them have to be put together suitably. This goes to make up the contents of the following sections 2.2 - 2.4, which in turn lay the ground for the correspondingly modular make-up of OSKAR to be discussed in sections 3.1 - 3.3 below.

Fig.3.   Semantic Form of DAdj as an INTERFACE between Linguistic and
                            Conceptual Structure

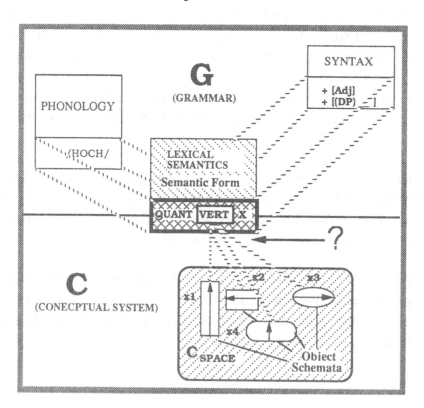

2.2 Dimension Assignment Parameters (DAPs): Their Origin, Nature, and Use

2.2.1 Categorization Grids

Technically speaking, the problem we face with DAPs is to specify the set of semantic constants which - when replacing the placeholder component DIM in (21) - yield appropriate semantic representations of the DAdjs at SF-level. The answer to this is easy to give by enumerating the DAPs as they are assumed in the theory under review as well as in OSKAR. For German DAdjs, we get the following list of (**bold faced**) DAPs inserted in the SF-schema in (21) and (pairs of) DAdjs which they represent:

(23)   SF-Representations of German DAdjs:

(a) [[QUANT **MAX** x]   =   [v $\pm$c]]   -   *lang - kurz*
(b) [[QUANT **ACROSS** d' x]   =   [v $\pm$c]][7]   -   *breit- schmal*
(c) [[QUANT **SUB** x]   =   [v $\pm$c]]   -   *dick - dünn*
(d) [[QUANT **DIST** x]   =   [v $\pm$c]]   -   *weit - eng*
(e) [[QUANT **VERT** x]   =   [v $\pm$c]]   -   *hoch - niedrig*
(f) [[QUANT **OBS** x]   =   [v +c]]   -   *tief*
(g) [[QUANT **FLACH** x]   =   [v +c]][8]   -   *flach*
(h) [[QUANT **SIZE** x]   =   [v $\pm$c]][9]   -   *groß - klein*

---

[7]   The Semantic Form of *breit - schmal* contains an additional argument variable d'. This is necessary to reflect the inherent relativity of this pair of DAdjs (the same holds for *wide-narrow*). In short, there is no independent defining spatial property according to which *breit -schmal* is assigned to physical objects. The object extent d to which *breit - schmal* is assigned is determined in relation to some other object extent d' where d' is identifiable independently as either length or height or depth. Cf. the examples in (18) and (19) above. - The peculiarity of this pair of DAdjs provides a striking argument in favour of the SF - CS distinction, but we cannot delve into this here (for details see Lang 1988, 1989).

[8]   Contrary to widely held views, *tief* does not have a lexical antonym in the same sense as have the DAdjs in (23)(a - e). *flach* is not the lexical antonym of *tief*. It is not even a DAdj but a somewhat differently structured Shape Adjective which - depending on context - may serve as a partial antonym to either *hoch* or *tief* or *steil* . The Semantic Form of *flach* contains a DAP similar to OBS of *tief* but with a different range of interpretation. For simplicity we use the label FLACH to conflate the specific componential structure of *flach*.

[9]   Actually, the Semantic Form of German *groß - klein* is a bit more complicated than represented here. For the purpose of the present paper, however, the DAP SIZE will do to cover the range of interpretations *groß - klein* may assume. (For a detailed discussion, cf. Lang 1987, 1989: Chap.5)

This list of DAPs is both necessary and sufficient to cope with the semantics of dimensional designation and positional variation. We wish to add just a few comments on the underlying principles.

First, each DAdj has exactly one representation at SF - level, but a range of interpretations on CS - level.

Second, this range of interpretations is determined by the conceptual module C_{SPACE} which organizes the way in which spatial objects are conceived.

Third, each spatial object x represents a certain ensemble of perceptually based and conceptually categorized properties. A subset of these properties is designated as **spatial dimensions** of x, that is, as gradable aspects of x which are at the same time relevant to human behaviour in the spatial environment of our terrestrial habitat.

For readers who are not just interested in the results but also in the way they have been gained, it might be rewarding to examine (23) in view of the following list of questions about the origin, nature, and use of the Dimension Assignment Parameters (DAPs):

(24)   How are these meaning components obtained and justified?
         What do they reveal about the way space perception is in-
         volved in the conceptualization of space?
         What defines some object x as a spatial object ?
         What are the dimensionable properties of x ?
         How are they to be represented at SF - level and CS - level?

Taking up the key words PERCEPTUALLY BASED and CONCEPTUALLY CATEGORIZED, we will briefly outline the notional components that provide answers to the questions listed in (24) above.

To begin with, some object x is defined as a **spatial object** by two interacting CATEGORIZATION GRIDS which are provisionally called **Inherent Proportion Schema (IPS)** and **Primary Perceptual Space (PPS)**. The former defines the dimensionable GESTALT PROPERTIES of a spatial object, the latter defines a system of axes within which the gestalt properties of objects can be interpreted as POSITION PROPERTIES. Take for instance the by now familiar examples in (25):

(25)   (a) *The pole is 10m* <u>*long*</u>   vs.   (b) *The pole is 10m* <u>*high*</u>

Long makes reference to the (perceptually salient) maximal extension of an object. Having a maximal axis is in any case a defining gestalt property, therefore *long* here identifies the maximal extension of a given pole. *High* in (25)(b) then interprets this maximal extension of the pole in terms of verticality thus turning the gestalt property into a position property. Speaking in terms of conceptual structure, we can put it like this:

(26)   An object *x* is assigned a POSITION PROPERTY if a certain axis extension of *x* defined by **IPS** is redefined by being projected onto an axis of the surrounding space as determined by **PPS**.

This projection is a directed one, revealing the asymmetry in the interaction of **IPS** and **PPS** which explains why (25)(b) entails (a), but not *vice versa* - cf. also (20) above. In short, dimensional designation of spatial objects rests crucially on identifying and interpreting object axes in terms of the two categorization grids **IPS** and **PPS**, which are determined by genetically anchored principles in the sense of Fig.1 above.

Now, after having briefly sketched what **IPS** and **PPS** are supposed to be, let us have a closer look at their internal structure. The grid called **IPS** is essentially based on categorizing visual input information according to a set of interacting principles. Without going into details (discussed at length in Lang 1987, 1989: Chap.3), we have to assume

(27)   PRINCIPLES OF OBJECT PERCEPTION
                 which determine

(i)   OBJECT DELIMITATION, - how the field of vision is analyzed into discernible bounded units which are defined by lines, edges, planes, and volumes.

(ii) SYMMETRY AXES, - how delimited objects are evaluated as to homogeneousness and orthogonality of their bounding surfaces in terms of the symmetry axes defining them. (Note that DAdjs pick out certain symmetry axes of an object *x* as reference extension.)

(iii) AXIAL DISINTEGRATION, - how symmetry-based object extensions are evaluated regarding discernibility within the given object. (Note that E. Rosch's 'basic level categories' *square, circle, triangle*, which are assessed to be optimal from the point of view of pattern recognition, are worst from the point of view of dimensional designation due to their lack of axial distinctness.)

(iv) SALIENCE/PROMINENCE, - how the axes specified so far are ordered within some object x according to their relative extent. This criterion singles out the maximal axis of x, if there is one, and arranges the extensions of x into a PROPORTION SCHEMA (hence the name given to this categorization grid).

(v) PENETRABILITY, - whether or not an object, due to certain SUB-STANCE PROPERTIES (poorly understood as yet), can be visually penetrated or not. It is this criterion which makes thickness a spatial property (albeit one where perceptual information is functionally interpreted) and which underlies the complementary distribution observed with *dick* [*thick*] and *weit* [*wide*] (in the sense of *wide on the inside*).

Obviously, there is some logical order within the five categorization steps (i) through (v) listed above. The first three lay the ground for any sort of dimensional designation, and are hence presupposed by all DAdjs - cf. Fig. 5 below. The fourth and the fifth categorization steps yield more specific features that differentiate among the DAdjs. Taken together, (27)(i) - (v) make up the categorization grid **IPS** which yields a subset of those parameters and values we need to come to grips with the semantics of dimensional designation, regarding both Semantic Form and CS repre-sentations.

As to Semantic Form, **IPS** provides us with the three Dimension Assignment Parameters MAX, SUB, DIST, which specify the dimensional meaning component of *lang - kurz, dick - dünn,* and *weit - eng,* respectively, in the way indicated in (23)(a,c,d) above. They are construed as **semantic primes** representing a set of conditions to identify an object extension, or more technically, as parameters on the SF - level which are instantiated at the CS - level. The CS representations providing the values which MAX, SUB, DIST can take are discussed in section 2.3 below.

Now let us turn to the other categorization grid called **Primary Perceptual Space (PPS)**. As one will guess from the name, **PPS** is meant as a model of space, specifically, as a model of how external physical space is conceptually reconstructed in terms of categorized sensory input delivered by our biological endowment. The relation of external physical space to this internal model of space is mediated by two steps of interpretation. Each of them involves modular interaction of autonomous systems along the lines indicated in section 2.1.1 above. <u>Sensory perception</u> emerges from how our senses instantiate physical parameters. In the case of spatial perception, it is above all those parameters which in one way or other derive from the force of gravity. The <u>conceptualization</u> of perceptual information involves categorization of perceptual input in view of its relevance to human behaviour. In other words, perceptive distinctions are conceptualized to just that extent that they are needed for the "naive physics" underlying our everyday knowledge of space. We will give an example of this in (28)(2) below.

While **IPS** is based almost exclusively on vision, **PPS** has a broader basis in drawing on perceptual input available from the organ of equilibrium, from upright posture, and from eye level. Each of these contributes a specific interpretation of external physical space. **PPS** consists of a set of principles that define three distinct axes. These, in turn, define our internal model of the external space. Otherwise we would not be able to discriminate between one-, two-, and three-dimensional objects. Therefore, **PPS** is fundamental to dimensional designation and positional variation of objects in space.

The relevant point is that the three axes of **PPS**, unlike the ones of a Cartesian system of coordinates, are rather unequal as to their origin and characteristics. It is these AXIAL PROPERTIES which are decisive for assigning spatial dimensions and positions to objects. We must refrain from spelling out the various perception-based principles that are involved in **PPS**. At any rate, what they produce is the following three axes (28)(1) - (3), each of which is being defined by a set of features evaluating the axis at issue with respect to (a) its <u>status</u> within **PPS**; (b) its specific axial <u>properties</u> (possibly reconstructible in terms of geometry); (c) its <u>relationship</u> to the other axes of **PPS**. As these characteristics form the real source of assigning spatial dimensions and positions to objects, we will have to go into them in more detail.

(28)   AXES defining PRIMARY PERCEPTUAL SPACE (**PPS** - Axes)

(28)(1)   VERTICAL AXIS (or for short: the Vertical).

(a) <u>Status</u>.   Originating from the effects of gravitation as perceived by
the organ of equilibrium, the Vertical is an orientation cue which is
ubiquitous and constant, that is, available everywhere in our terrestrial
habitat and with the same effect at all times. This makes verticality a
primary cue of spatial perception to the effect that, within **PPS**, the
Vertical is granted the status of an **independent** axis.

(b) <u>Properties</u>.   Man's upright posture assigns the Vertical a natural
foot on the earth's surface (or on a parallel plane that serves as ground
level) and a **fixed direction** which is determined as **geofugal** by the top-
bottom asymmetry of the human body. In geometrical terms, the Vertical
thus has the attributes of a ray or directed segment. The foot serves as a
zero-point F such that any points F', F''(distinct from F) on the Vertical
define directed segments that increase unidirectionally. The direction
defined by F, F', F''... etc. corresponds to the direction of the height scale
whose intervals are construed as increasing degrees of height assigned to
the objects in question.

(c) <u>Relationship</u>.   Based on (a) and (b), the Vertical is physically as well
as conceptually the most salient and also the dominant axis of **PPS**; the
other axes are defined in relation to the Vertical. We will see that the
submodule C_{SPACE} is pervaded with characteristics owing to the Vertical's
dominance.

Vertical **dimension** vs. vertical **distance**. Notice that the Vertical is the
common basis for both the dimensional (or extensional) use and the so-
called distance (or positional) use of the adjectives *high - low*. The
difference consists, among other things, in the way in which the points F,
F', F'' of the Vertical are instantiated by objects said to be *high* or *low*. The
picture in Fig. 4 below illustrates the two interpretations of a sentence like
The window is 2 m high [10].

---

10   In many languages, the distinction between Dimension and Distance interpretation
of *high -low* is grammaticalized. Thus in French the example has two translations:
(i)   *La fenêtre est haute* (dimension interpretation, gender agreement of the adjective)
(ii)   *La fenêtre est haut* (distance interpretation, no gender agreement of the adjective)

Fig. 4   Dimension vs. Distance Interpretation of *high (window)*

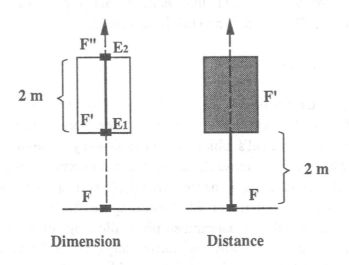

The Dimension Interpretation of *high - low* involves the projection of two axis endpoints E_1 and E_2 onto the Vertical such that the segment formed by $\overline{E_1E_2}$ is transformed into a directed segment defined by the points $\overline{F'F''}$ of the Vertical. The deciding condition of this interpretation is that the relevant points of the Vertical, i.e. F', F", are instantiated by axial endpoints of one and the same object x. In contrast, the Distance Interpretation of *high - low* is based on the condition that the points F', F"of the Vertical are instantiated by distinct objects. In the given example it is the window as a whole which is projected onto F', thereby defining the directed segment $\overrightarrow{FF'}$ of the Vertical as a distance between ground level and window. In short, the Dimension Interpretation is based on a directed segment <u>defined within one object</u>, whereas the Distance Interpretation is based on a directed segment <u>defined between objects</u>. Although the Dimension and Distance Interpretations of *high - low* obviously make reference to the same **PPS** axis, the Vertical, they have to be analysed as distinct devices of spatial orientation. The Distance Interpretation still awaits careful analysis.

For the time being, OSKAR is designed to account for all facts of the Dimension Interpretation of DAdjs. With this in mind, we may conclude the brief discussion of the Vertical by making the following claim. The conceptual relevance of F and F' as points on the Vertical rests on the fact

---

For more details on the Distance Interpretation see Lang 1987, 1989 Chap. 2

that they serve as location parameters to be invariably instantiated by asymmetric (pairs of) concepts like "bottom" and "top", "lower end" and "upper end" etc. We will return to this in section 2.2.3.

(28)(2)   OBSERVER AXIS.

(a) Status.   Originating in the visual organ, this axis is determined by the line of sight of a (potential or actual) observer. Because of this it is - in contrast to the Vertical's ubiquity and constancy - **flexible in two respects.** First, having a movable source (i.e. the observer), this axis does not have a fixed anchorage in the surrounding physical space but is induced by a moving human interpreter of physical space. Second, the Observer Axis has an anatomically determined pivot allowing for a 180° turn in either of two planes (vertically and horizontally). Being the axis of depth perception, the Observer Axis certainly provides another pillar of spatial perception. However, due to the fact that the Observer Axis is bound to human carriers whose normal position (upright posture) is defined in re- lation to the surrounding physical space, this axis is **not** as **independent** an axis within **PPS** as is the Vertical. We will see the consequences of this in section 2.2.3 below.

(b) Properties.   Defined by a (real or imaginary) observer's gaze, the Observer Axis has a **direction** which is biologically fixed as **away from the observer,** and it has a **bounding point O**, which (disregarding disparity) is given by the anatomically determined origin of an observer's line of sight.
In geometrical terms, the Observer Axis can also be described as a ray or directed segment. It is defined by the bounding point **O** and has a direction in that any points **O'**, **O"** determine unidirectionally increasing distances from **O**. Drawing on this, the Observer Axis provides the scale basis for DEPTH ASSIGNMENT.

Originating in the visual organ of a human observer, however, the Observer Axis of **PPS** simultaneously serves other purposes as well. Thus it also forms the basis for perspectivizing spatial objects. PERSPECTIV- IZATION consists of assigning objects observer-determined "fronts" and "backs" etc. and locating objects x, y relative to one another, as in x *is in front of* y or y *is behind* x etc. In short, the Observer Axis is the carrier of two major cognitive cues of spatial orientation: DEPTH ASSIGNMENT and PERSPECTIVIZATION. We will return to these immediately below.

(c)   Relationship.   In the unmarked case, given by the position of the eyes of an observer in upright posture, the Observer Axis is orthogonal (at 90°) to the Vertical. In the other relevant configuration, the Vertical and the Observer Axis lie at an angle of 180° such that they run parallel but in diametrically opposed directions. The third case, where the Vertical and the Observer Axis run in the same direction (at 0°), is perceptually quite conceivable but, interestingly enough, does not constitute a conceptually relevant parameter. There are data[11] which prove that this kind of doubly determined axis identification is not utilized semantically.

As mentioned above, the Observer Axis of **PPS** serves the purposes of DEPTH ASSIGNMENT and PERSPECTIVIZATION. Coming from the same biological source, these two cognitive devices closely interact with respect to the assignments they deliver. Note, however, that DEPTH ASSIGNMENT and PERSPECTIVIZATION are partially independent in that they draw on distinct spatial structures; therefore, they have to be analyzed separately.

Regarding DEPTH ASSIGNMENT by means of DAdjs such as *tief* [*deep*], we have to distinguish between Dimension and Distance Interpretations. The analogy to Verticality assignment by means of *high-low* discussed in (28)(1) above is not accidental, but reveals just another facet of the crucial role of the **PPS**-axes in the organization of spatial knowledge. The Observer Axis serves to assign depth to objects (in both interpretations of *deep*) only if the objects can be conceived as "crossing the obverver's gaze". It is exactly on this condition that the relevant points of the Observer Axis, that is, the bounding point **O** and its successors **O'**, **O''**, can be

---

[11]   Just as an indication, we wish to quote the following documented example

(i)   *The rocket rose into height and disappeared in the depth of space*

The fact that the visible path of the rocket covers one continuous segment (simultaneously determined by the Vertical and the Observer Axis running equidirectionally) cannot be semantically accommodated in one DAdj. Instead, the semantic structure of DAdjs necessitates a way of designating the path of the rocket which construes the relevant projections as concatenated, the point of linkage being marked by a shift in the reference system (from **PPS** to the universe).

furnished with the appropriate instantiations needed for DEPTH ASSIGNMENT. As with *high-low,* the distinct interpretations of *deep* result from whether the points **O'** and **O"** are instantiated by axial endpoints of one and the same object *x* (= Dimension Interpretation) or by distinct objects *x, y* (= Distance Interpretation).

There are further differences to be observed, including various peculiarities of the Distance Interpretation of *deep*. For instance, *deep* may also occur as a modifier of a prepositional phrase headed by *in* , cf. *Tarzan lives deep in the jungle* or *Jane ran deep into the forest.* In such cases, distance is defined on the basis of local inclusion: the object to be located ("Tarzan", "Jane") is conceived as being contained in the reference object ("jungle", "forest"). We will not delve into this here, but rather depict the common basis of both types of interpretation for *deep* in Fig. 5.

Fig. 5   Dimension vs. Distance Interpretation of *deep*

The box is 2 m deep / in depth

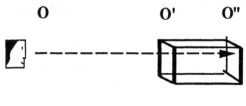

Dimension

The ball lies / is deeper in the basket than the triangle

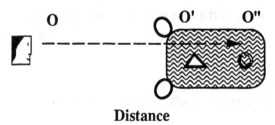

Distance

PERSPECTIVIZATION will be touched upon only to the extent that it concerns the assignment of observer-determined sides to objects. There are basically two strategies for assigning observer-related sides to an object which does not have any intrinsically fixed front-back distinction. Each of these strategies corresponds to a specific spatial situation defined by the observer's location with respect to the object(s) at issue. Following familiar terminology (e.g. Herskovits 1986: Chap.10), one is called the ENCOUNTER SITUATION - the observer faces the object from a distance; the other is called the COINCIDENCE SITUATION - the observer transfers his own front-back distinction onto the object in question.

Consider the situations according to which an object, say, a block, is assigned "front" (F) and "back" (B), and how, depending on that, a ball and a triangle are located in relation to the block. Figure 6 below shows the relevant spatial configurations of observer, objects, and observer-related object sides.

Fig. 6   Perspectivization and Side Assignment

ENCOUNTER SITUATION

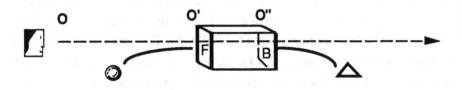

COINCIDENCE SITUATION

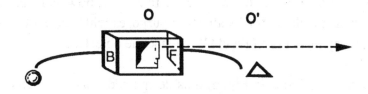

While the bounding point O of the Observer Axis is given by the observer in a like manner for both situations, there is an important difference between the two situations as to the role of the successor points O', O".
In the ENCOUNTER SITUATION, point O' is instantiated by the less distant object face, which is then designated as "front" (F) or "accessible face"; O" is instantiated by the more distant object face, which is designated as "back" (B) or "remote face". Note the analogy to the Dimension Interpretation of *deep* in Fig. 5 above.

Thus, according to this strategy, "front" and "back" are assigned to an object in terms of increasing distance from **O** on the Observer Axis. This is the source of the well-known MIRROR EFFECT of assigning an object an observer-determined front.

Given this, we have the appropriate side-determined regions (surrounding the block) at our disposal, in reference to which the ball is said to be *in front of*, and the triangle *in back of* or *behind*, the block. The crucial feature of this strategy of assigning observer-related sides and side-related locations to objects lies in the fact that the concepts "front" and "back" consistently correlate with less distant and more distant object faces, respectively. Hence, the relational concepts derived from them, "in front of" and "in back of" or "behind", are transitive relations and are converses of each other.

In the COINCIDENCE SITUATION, however, the crucial point is that the object *x,* to which sides are assigned, <u>coincides</u> with the observer her/himself in instantiating the bounding point **O** (cf. Fig. 6). This has the effect that the Observer Axis originating from **O** is no longer relevant to assigning sides to the object *x,* which itself instantiates **O**. According to this strategy, then, the assignment to objects of observer-related "fronts" and "backs" is not a projection of object sides onto points **O', O"** of the Observer Axis, but a projection of the observer's intrinsic front and back onto the object in question - hence the altered distribution of "front" and "back" with respect to the block in Fig. 6. Even under this view, however, the Observer Axis remains available for localisation purposes with respect to any objects *y, z* that may instantiate **O'** and **O"** outside the object *x* .

Now, if the block in Fig. 6, thus designated, serves as reference object for locating the other objects, then the ball is said to be *in back of* or *behind*, and the triangle *in front of*, the block. This assignment is the reverse of the one we would obtain according to the ENCOUNTER SITUATION. The difference between ENCOUNTER and COINCIDENCE SITUATIONS, as concerns side assignment, can be reduced to the distinct instantiations of **O**, that is, either an object side facing the observer or the observer himself[12]. If this is

---

12   There are a couple of questions left open, of course. The outline given here is confined to those aspects that are immediately relevant to the assignment of sides and locations to objects as modelled in OSKAR.

granted, the assignment based on COINCIDENCE can be regarded as a special case of the assignment based on the ENCOUNTER SITUATION. This, in turn, supports the claim that, concerning the assignment of observer-related sides to objects, the **PPS**-axes approach presented here allows for more generalizations than the observer-centered approach proposed by e.g. Herskovits 1986, 1988. Speaking of the Observer Axis, there is also the much-discussed distinction between DEICTICALLY and INTRINSICALLY assigned "fronts" and "backs" etc., which in connexion with conditions on PERSPECTIVIZATION can also be traced to the same distinction, see section 2.2.3.

(28)(3)   HORIZONTAL AXIS.

(a) <u>Status</u>.   This third axis of **PPS** is not an axis we are equipped to identify by primary perceptual information, but is **derived from**, hence **dependent on**, the two others just to fill the gap determined by the properties of the latter.

(b) <u>Properties</u>.   Based on this, the Horizontal does **not** have **any bounding points** or **directions**. Geometrically, it is reduced to the attributes of a simple line. This is the source of the well-known difficulties in distinguishing "left" from "right". When an object axis is assigned horizontality, its endpoints E and E' are left unspecified with respect to instantiations of "left" or "right". All that can be said about side assignment is that E and E' may not get the same value. The distribution of "left" and "right" on the sides of an object, however, is (partially) dependent on the side assignments the object receives due to its verticality and/or its observer-determined "front" - "back" features.

(c) <u>Relationship</u>.   Physically supported by the earth's surface and visually perceivable due to the flexibility of the observer's gaze (cf. (28)(2)(a)), the Horizontal is exclusively defined by its **orthogonality** to the Vertical and to the Observer Axis.

The **PPS** also functions as a categorization grid which, like **IPS**, yields values and parameters for the identification of POSITION PROPERTIES of spatial objects in the sense of (26) above. Regarding the Semantic Forms of DAdjs, **PPS** provides us with the parameters VERT, OBS and FLACH, which account for the dimensional meaning of *hoch - niedrig* [*high - low, tall*], *tief* [*deep*], and *flach*, respectively.

The perceptual basis and the conceptual categorization of these DAPs is summarized in Fig. 7 .

Fig.7   Justifying/Deriving Conceptual Distinctions in Spatial Objects

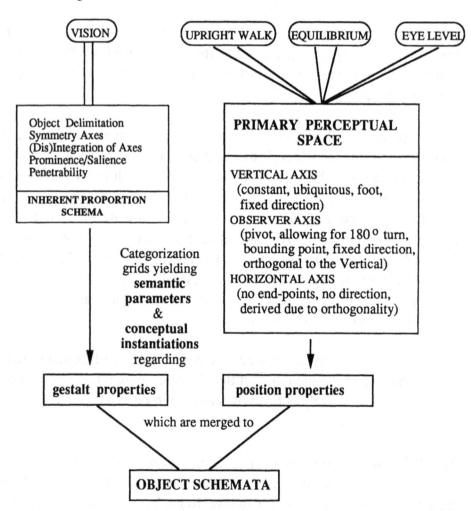

Physical Preconditions:
Physical Space, Light, Gravitation, Organisms

PERCEPTUAL LEVEL

Biological Endowment

VISION   UPRIGHT WALK   EQUILIBRIUM   EYE LEVEL

Object Delimitation
Symmetry Axes
(Dis)Integration of Axes
Prominence/Salience
Penetrability

INHERENT PROPORTION
SCHEMA

PRIMARY PERCEPTUAL
SPACE

VERTICAL AXIS
 (constant, ubiquitous, foot,
 fixed direction)
OBSERVER AXIS
 (pivot, allowing for 180° turn,
 bounding point, fixed direction,
 orthogonal to the Vertical)
HORIZONTAL AXIS
 (no end-points, no direction,
 derived due to orthogonality)

Categorization
grids yielding
semantic
parameters
&
conceptual
instantiations
regarding

gestalt properties   position properties

which are merged to

OBJECT SCHEMATA

CONCEPTUAL LEVEL

2.2.2   Inventory of DAPs

To show that things like MAX, SUB etc. are not mere labels, but theoretical constructs having a clear-cut interpretation within the scope of the theory, the conditions encoded in each of these DAPs may be spelled out like this:

MAX   identifies the most extended disintegrated axis of some object x, which in turn presupposes that there is exactly one such axis of x available (remember the inapplicability of *lang - kurz* (*long - short*) to circles or squares).

SUB   identifies either a non-maximal disintegrated third axis (cf. *thick board, thin slice of bread*) or an integrated axis forming the diameter of a circular section (cf. *thick pole, thin stick*).

DIST   identifies an object axis perceived as inside diameter of a hollow body. Thus, though SUB and DIST identify the same type of axis in terms of geometry, they draw on mutually exclusive perceptual properties in terms of the theory underlying our everyday knowledge of spatial objects. SUB refers to axes determined by solid (parts of) objects, DIST to axes determined by hollow ones.

VERT   selects, if assigned via *hoch* or *tall* etc. to some spatial object x, exactly that disintegrated axis of x which coincides with the Vertical of **PPS**. By way of projection the object axis thus identified inherits some or all of the axial properties of the Vertical noted in (28)(1) above.

OBS   selects, if assigned via *tief* to some spatial object x, any disintegrated axis of x which coincides with the Observer axis of **PPS**. Again, assigning OBS (or its variant FLACH) to an object axis is tantamount to transferring some or all of the properties of the Observer axis, noted in (28)(2) above, to the object axis concerned.

ACROSS   designates a disintegrated object axis which is left unspecified by any of the other DAPs referring to maximality, substance, verticality, or alignment to the Observer Axis. As stated in (28)(3) above, the third axis of **PPS** does not yield a parameter of its own. This gap is partially filled by the derived parameter ACROSS which accounts for the inherent relativity of *breit - schmal* (*wide, broad - narrow*) discussed in Fn. 7. Notice that ACROSS is a stop-gap with respect to both **IPS** and **PPS**. Within **PPS**, ACROSS covers horizontality, that is, it is assigned to an axis to which neither VERT nor OBS apply; within **IPS**, ACROSS supplements the parameters MAX and SUB in that it is assigned to an axis to which neither of these applies.

To sum up: it is this small set of semantic parameters which controls the way in which natural languages assign spatial dimensions and positions to objects. The efficiency and flexibility of the linguistic system in general is based on modularity (cf. 2.1.1). As regards the specific subset at issue, the flexibility of dimensional designation rests on the fact that each of the Dimension Assignment Parameters (DAPs) presented above has a certain range of values instantiating it at the conceptual level (henceforth called: DIMENSION ASSIGNMENT VALUES or DAVs). The efficiency of dimensional designation is due to the fact that the DAPs do not simply have disjoint ranges of DAVs at the level of conceptual interpretation. Rather, they interact to define a structured domain of values at CS - level, where some DAPs have overlapping, some DAPs have including, and some DAPs have complementary ranges of DAVs. Given this, we may go one step further by claiming that the domain of DAVs at CS - level is structured by conditions on mapping DAPs onto CS - level. These conditions are illustrated by the facts presented in (10) - (15) and by examples such as (18)-(20), and they are informally expressed in the characteristics of the DAPs given above.

The questions that arise at this point read: What are the representational entities at CS - level onto which the DAPs are mapped? What are the conditions on this mapping? Needless to say, these are interdependent problems. The first relates to how objects are represented conceptually, the second to how dimensional designation works to identify or to specify object concepts. On heuristic grounds, we will tackle the second first by reviewing the various types of ORIENTATION and/or PERSPECTIVIZATION exemplified in (14) and (15) above. This will give us some instructive information about the structure of object concepts, about how they are stored and retrieved, and about how they are possibly modified in actual contexts of use.

2.2.3   Types of Orientation and Perspectivization of Objects

For clarity of exposition, we will start by repeating the sample of data presented in (14) and (15), and then continue by explicating the various types of reference to the surrounding space in terms of DAPs and DAVs. Recall the following (=(14)):

(29)   The distribution of *hoch* subdivides 3D objects into four subclasses of objects with respect to having[13]

	(a) fixed orientation	(mountain, river)
	(b) canonical orientation	(tower, desk)
	(c) inherent orientation	(book, picture)
or	(d) being unspecified as to orientation	(brick, pole)

Reformulated in terms of DAPs we may put it like that: applying the semantic parameter VERT encoded in *hoch - niedrig* to objects is tantamount to designating an object axis as being aligned to the Vertical. In view of the distinctions listed in (29)(a) - (d), however, there seem to be four ways of relating an object axis to the Vertical, or, to put it in another way, there seem to be four ways according to which an object axis is assigned verticality.

Now, as stated in 2.2.2 above, if VERT is assigned to an object x it selects a certain disintegrated axis of x , thereby transferring some or all of the properties of the Vertical to this object axis. If this is correct, then the four distinct cases of assigning verticality to objects should be traceable to distinct ways of transferring properties of the Vertical to an object axis. And this is indeed the case, as will be shown immediately in (30)(a) - (d) below.

Note that in view of the properties of the Vertical stated in (28)(1) above, assigning verticality to an object axis is inseparably linked with specifying the position of the object at issue with respect to **PPS**. If an

---

[13]   The terms *canonical* and *inherent* resemble the terminology introduced by Lyons (1977: 697ff.), but the labels used here are different as to their distribution as well as to their interpretation. The relevant issue, however, seems to be that Lyons' differentiation is much coarser than the one proposed here.

object x is said to have an ORIENTATION, this means that x has a position assigned to it which is determined by the way x is located in **PPS** in relation to the Vertical. The assignment of verticality features thus reveals the intrinsic relation between an object's position and its location in space. This, by the way, is but one aspect of the dominant role of the Vertical regarding the conceptualization of space. With this in mind we will now briefly examine the different types of orientation occurring with objects. We will discuss three types of intrinsic orientation first, then turn to contextually induced orientation.

(30)(a)   FIXED ORIENTATION

An object x is said to have a fixed orientation if x has an axis which **shares all of the properties of the Vertical** listed in (28)(1)(a, b), specifically, if the foot **F** of the Vertical located on the earth's surface is instantiated as the "bottom" of x, without any shift or projection. This, of course, restricts the class of objects which x may be an element of to those objects which in a way form material shells or embodiments of the Vertical *per se*. Therefore, the objects that have a fixed orientation are designated parts of the earth's surface, folded upwards, which are either natural (mountain, hill, dune) or man-made (rampart, embankment).

Being conceived of as material embodiments of the Vertical implies that these objects do have both a fixed position and location within **PPS**, i.e., they cannot be moved or displaced or tilted over etc. In short: **fixed orientation correlates with immobility**. Both are non-detachable features of the conceptual representation of the objects concerned.

(30)(b)   CANONICAL ORIENTATION

An object x is said to have a canonical orientation if x has an axis which is assigned verticality on the basis of **transferring the properties of the Vertical** listed in (28)(1)(b) to an axis of x. The mapping is defined by a function C which takes the end-points E, E' of the object axis as arguments and yields the specified end-points B and T as values, where B and T are interpreted as **fixed projections** of the points F and F' of the Vertical. Thus, F projected onto E yields B, which is instantiated by "bottom"; while E' (which, due to the transfer of the geofugal direction of the Vertical, is an projection of F') is specified as T yielding "top".

Canonical verticality rests on the fact that the projection of **F** and **F'** onto the end-points E and E' of an object axis is conceived as a fixed prolongation of the Vertical into the object x. Verticality, thus assigned, implies the objects concerned to be simultaneously assigned a normal position which is defined in reference to the Vertical of the surrounding space. Objects having a canonical orientation may thus of course be moved, turned around, tilted over etc. but any position of theirs not meeting the conditions of fixed projection has to be judged as marked (*e.g.* a desk standing upside down) or even deviant (e.g. a tower lying after having toppled down, as suggested by *long tower*). In short, having canonical orientation is part of the conceptual representation of the objects concerned.

(30)(c)   INHERENT ORIENTATION

An object x is said to have an inherent orientation if x has an axis which is assigned verticality in a way similar to the one described in (30)(b) - but with the crucial difference that "top" and "bottom" are instantiated in the object's own right, that is, that the inherent height of object x no longer has any links with the Vertical of the surrounding space. Thus a book, for instance, has an inherent height (and therefore inherent "top", "bottom", "beginning", "end") due to the inscription it carries. Likewise, a photograph showing Heike and a button showing Gorbi have an **inherent verticality** which is maintained absolutely **independent of the object's actual position** (standing, lying, hanging upside down etc.).

Inherent verticality of an object is thus to be conceived as a way of orientation which, though originally being derived from the Vertical due to pragmatic conditions, has become independent of the axes of **PPS**. This explains why a difference between intrinsic and actual verticality of an object x, say, if x is tipped over, can produce quite distinct results as to conceptualization. To imagine a mountain as tipped over or standing on edge is almost impossible; to conceive a tower as long (i.e. as lying down) involves cutbacks on the concept "tower"; whereas to see a book lying on the table or standing upside down does not at all affect our understanding of "book". At best, the difference between inherent and actual verticality of a book may be taken as indicator of a pragmatic deviation.

(30)(d)   CONTEXTUALLY INDUCED ORIENTATION

An object x is said to have a contextually induced orientation if x has an axis which is assigned verticality in a way similar to the one described in (30)(b) - but with the difference that the projection of **F** and **F'** onto the endpoints E and E' of an axis of some object x, and therefore the instantiation of "bottom" and "top", apply to the **actual position** of the object at issue. Verticality can be induced contextually with objects that in themselves are unspecified as to orientation (cf. a long pole specified as *tall pole,* a brick specified as being *17 cm in height* etc.) or that have an inherent orientation. The latter case causes the multiple interpretation of *e.g. The tombstone is too high to fit into the trunk*, where *high* can either refer to the tombstone's inherent top - bottom extent or to its contextually specified thickness. With objects having a canonical orientation, con-textually induced verticality makes sense only if the object at issue is not in normal position. Otherwise, the DAP VERT (cf. *tall tower, low table*) will in any case be instantiated by the canonically oriented object axis.

Contextually induced orientation thus amounts to specifying the **actual position of an object with reference to the Vertical.** Normally, this applies to freely movable objects which do not have an intrinsic (fixed or canonical) orientation. At the conceptual level, the difference between intrinsic and contextually induced orientation reappears in the way the DAP VERT is instantiated at CS-level: in the first case an intrinsic verticality feature of an object axis is **identified**, in the second case a suitable object axis is **specified** by inducing a verticality feature.

Moving on to PERSPECTIVIZATION we find a very similar picture, except that there seems to be one type of assignment missing with OBS. Recall again the data in (15), repeated here as (31):

(31)   The distribution of *tief* subdivides 3D objects into three subclasses
           of objects with respect to having
                      (a) canonical perspectivization   (river, cupboard)
                      (b) inherent perspectivization   (hole, wound)
           or   (c) being unspecified as to perspective (brick, board)

The first point to note is that here there is no analogue to fixed orientation in (30)(a). We argue that this is caused by the fact that the Observer Axis differs from the Vertical in a couple of features, as stated in (28)(2). What is different, to begin with, is the way in which perspectivization (that is, interpreting the DAP OBS with respect to some spatial object x) relates to the specification of the object's position and to its mobility characteristics. Unlike the Vertical, the Observer Axis is not constant and independent, but flexible in two respects. It has a pivot allowing for a 180° turn in the vertical and the horizontal plane, and it has a moving source which - taking upright posture as normal position - is at least partially determined by its relation to the Vertical.

This has the consequence that there is no way of assigning an object a fixed perspective in exactly the same sense as an object may have a fixed orientation. It takes but a moment's reflection to see why. In view of the flexibility of the Observer Axis, it holds that the position it assigns to an object is also determined by the position of the observer. Hence there cannot be any object x which embodies depth in such a way that this alone would suffice to locate x in the surrounding space and simultaneously determine its position. Note the rule: **Perspectivization is always linked with orientation.** So much as to why the analogue of FIXED ORIENTATION is missing with DEPTH ASSIGNMENT.

(32)(a)   CANONICAL PERSPECTIVIZATION

An object x is said to have a canonical perspectivization with respect to the Observer if x, on account of its intrinsic orientation according to (30)(a) or (b), also has an axis that is designated as being aligned to the Observer's line of sight. Based on the fact that there are two relevant angles at which the Observer Axis may run to the Vertical - cf. (28)(2)(c), we have to distinguish two cases of canonical perspectivization.

The first case is exemplified by objects such as cupboard or doorway, where the depth axis is orthogonal to the canonically assigned vertical axis. These objects are movable but have a canonical position determined by their orientation and, depending on that, by their perspectivization. The mapping of O and O' onto the endpoints E and E' of the axis concerned follows the ENCOUNTER strategy (shown in Fig. 6) in such a way that O is mapped onto E and instantiated as canonical "front"; O' is mapped onto E' and instantiated as canonical "back".

The second case is exemplified by objects such as river, ditch or well, where the depth axis runs at an angle of 180° to the Vertical, that is, the object axis designated as depth axis continues the Vertical from F in the opposite direction ("downward"). The function D that maps the bounding point O of the Observer Axis onto the foot F of the Vertical and takes account of the opposite directions in an appropriate way is discussed at length in Lang 1987, 1989: Chap. 2. Note that the immobility of objects such as river or ditch is due to their having a fixed orientation in the sense of (30)(a), that is, a fixed relation to the Vertical similar to objects such as mountain or rampart. Thus, mountain and river group together in being designated parts of the earth's surface, and therefore being immobile objects, but they differ in their relation to the Observer Axis.

The fact that the depth axis assigned to a river continues the Vertical in the opposite direction does have its consequences regarding the mapping of O and O' onto the endpoints of the object axis at issue. In short: the mapping also follows the ENCOUNTER strategy described above, but with the additional effect (induced by the Vertical) that O, when mapped onto E, is instantiated as "accessible surface" (which conflates "top" and "front"); while O', when mapped onto E', is instantiated as "ground" (which conflates "bottom" and "remote face").

This view of CANONICAL PERSPECTIVIZATION seems to match with the way depth is conceptualized, not least due to the fact that it reflects the dominant role of the Vertical and the subsidiary role of the Observer Axis.

(32)(b)   INHERENT PERSPECTIVIZATION

An object x is said to have an inherent perspectivization if x has a disintegrated axis which can only be identified by being aligned to the Observer Axis. In other words, if there are no other cues available for assigning x a position property (by relating the axis at issue to the Vertical) or for assigning x a maximal or substance-determined axis, then precisely this object axis is designated as depth.

Note that, in line with INHERENT ORIENTATION in (30)(b), the notion of INHERENT PERSPECTIVIZATION is basically defined as "assigning an axis of object *x* the properties of an axis of **PPS** without regard to the object's actual position in space". Regarding inherent depth, this is exactly the case with either immobile hollow objects, *e.g.* holes, or freely movable objects with an interior, *e.g.* cups, pots, bottles etc. A (non-perforated) hole, no matter whether it is in the floor, in the wall, or in the ceiling, is invariably assigned depth. As the example suggests, a hole or the interior of a cup is conceived as a designated (negative or missing) part of the solid object containing it. Therefore, a hole or the interior of a cup cannot move or change position by itself. Given this, it is due to the flexibility of the Observer Axis that such objects can be inherently assigned depth without regard to their location in the surrounding space.

The mapping of **O** and **O'** onto E and E' proceeds along the lines of the ENCOUNTER - based strategy described in (28)(2)(b) above, that is, **O** is mapped onto E and instantiated as "front" or "accessible surface"; while **O'** is mapped onto E' and instantiated as "ground" or "remote face".

(32)(c)   CONTEXTUALLY INDUCED PERSPECTIVIZATION

An object *x* is said to have a contextually induced perspectivization if *x* has an axis which is assigned depth due only to the **actual position** of the object at issue, that is, if neither (32)(a) nor (32)(b) apply. Depth can be induced contextually with objects which in themselves are unspecified as to perspectivization and which at the same time have a disintegrated axis that can be aligned to the Observer Axis. The latter condition rules out the possibility of assigning objects like ball, rod, or tower depth as a dimension (cf. **The ball is 15cm in depth*)[14]

As discussed in (28)(2)(b) above, there are two ways of mapping **O** and **O'** onto the endpoints of the object axis that is designated as depth axis. This claim would predict that contextual perspectivization, when applied to objects that in themselves are unspecified as to perspectivization, should yield to different assignments of "front" (or "accessible face") and "back" (or "remote face") emerging from either the ENCOUNTER SITUATION or

---

14   Though, of course, the Observer Axis is the basis of assigning a ball etc. a contextually determined "front view". Within OSKAR this is accounted for by the auxiliary DAV diam which unlike vert or obs is not the conceptual instantiation of a dimensional expression from (8),(9) but of *diameter* . The axis forming the diameter of a circular section is never designated as depth but it can yield endpoints that may be instantiations of **O** and **O'** of the Observer Axis.

the COINCIDENCE SITUATION. And this is indeed the case. The choice between these depends on contextual cues and/or on language-particular options of linguistic coding. We will come back to this immediately.

The different ways of perspectivizing an object discussed so far are closely related to the familiar distinction of INTRINSIC vs. DEICTIC assignment of sides to objects. As can be seen easily, objects that have a CANONICAL or INHERENT PERSPECTIVIZATION along the lines of (32)(a) and (b), have, in consequence, INTRINSICALLY determined "fronts" and "backs" (or, "accessible surfaces" and "remote faces"), construed as instantiations of the end-points of that object axis that is designated as being aligned to the Observer Axis. Given this, it is up to CONTEXTUALLY INDUCED PERSPECTIVIZATION to account for DEICTICALLY determined "fronts" and "backs".

Now, as concerns the different assignments possible within this scope (recall the discussion in (28)(2)(b)), there seem to be linguistically based differences. So Hill (1982) has pointed out that Hausa prefers a way of assigning deictic "fronts" that would correspond to the COINCIDENCE SITUATION (cf. (28)(2)(b)(ii) above, also known as the "tandem-principle"). On the other hand, there is strong evidence that German, English and their cognates encode deictic assignment of "fronts" and "backs" according to the ENCOUNTER SITUATION described in (28)(2)(b)(i) above. Therefore, within the framework of OSKAR, the interpretation of deictic "fronts" and "backs" will be **restricted to this type** of assignment.

So much for the ways in which objects are assigned dimensions and positions simultaneously. Based on this it seems reasonable to restrict the distinctive attributes FIXED, INHERENT, and CANONICAL vs. CON-TEXTUALLY INDUCED to the scope of position properties that derive from **PPS** parameters. With one exception, related to what might be called

(33)   INHERENT LENGTH

There is some sense in claiming a similar (though slightly different) distinction also regarding the assignment of length to an object due to the maximality parameter of **IPS**. In view of the characteristics given to the DAP MAX in 2.2.2 above, an object axis designated as length has to be identifiable as the maximal axis. This implies that an object axis designated as length should in any case also represent the actual maximal. Basically, this is right. But there are classes of objects which may contain elements the length axis of which need not be the actual maximal axis. Take a double bed or a drill (farming machinery) that may be wider than long as regards their actual proportion. In both cases, the object's length axis is primarily determined by functional parameters, say, "alignment to the length of the human body" or "alignment to the axis of motion". Based on this, such objects may have an INHERENT LENGTH AXIS which need not coincide with their actual maximal axis.

After this short digression, we wish to summarize the facts presented in this subsection. Dimensional designation of objects, as far as it draws on relating certain object axes to the axes of **PPS**, has been shown to be intricately linked with assigning position properties to objects with reference to the surrounding space. More precisely, within the general device of relating an object axis to the Vertical and/or the Observer Axis, we have to distinguish four types of relations each of which is determined by a specific set of properties that is transferred from the **PPS** axis at issue to the object axis concerned. Roughly divided into ORIENTATION and PERSPECTIVIZATION, this transfer of properties from **PPS**-axes to object axes results in distinct types of verticality and/or depth assignment that are conceptually crucial. As a matter of fact, it is fundamental to our conceptual knowledge of an object x (i.e. the concept "x"), whether or not x has intrinsically assigned position properties, and if so, which ones. And it is likewise fundamental to our conceptualization of space that the axes of **PPS** define the general location frame within which objects are assigned dimensions and positions.

In other words, the types of verticality and/or depth assignment discussed in (28) - (32) and the principles according to which these assignments interact in determining the crucial features of object concepts, form the substantial basis of the interdependence of spatial knowledge and object knowledge as outlined in (A) and (B) at the beginning of this paper.

We summarize the facts about verticality and/or depth assignments and their interrelations to an object's (im-)mobility by the following diagram shown in Fig. 8. To give an indication of what it really means, some brief comments seem to be in order.

First,   for the purpose of transparency, the division of objects into immobile objects and movable objects is indicated by ▨ dotted and white backgrounding, respectively. Notice, however, that these mobility characteristics are not independent, but ensue from the values each object assumes regarding boundedness, dimensionality, and relation to PPS-axes.

Second, the terminal nodes of the taxonomy, thus determined, are exemplified by illustrative samples of object concepts. They give an idea of what information is included in the Object Schemata (cf. section 2.3).

Third, the categorization of objects in Fig. 8 is designed to account for the range of conditions according to which the DAPS VERT and OBS are instantiated by values at the CS - level. The division of spatial objects into four classes, that is, immobile objects, on the one hand, and three classes of movable objects, on the other, directly reflects the range of positional variation each of these classes of objects can be submitted to. Put in terms of, say, *lying, standing, tilted over* etc., the following holds: immobile objects do not allow for any variation of their position; canonically oriented objects allow for changes in their verticality assigment (a tower can be said to *lie* after having toppled down; roots can be said to *lie* where they were extracted from the bed; a shelf can stand *upside down* etc.); inherently oriented objects allow for all changes of position (*lying, standing, upside down*); and so do contextually oriented and/or perspectivized objects, but not all possible changes of position are concept–ually relevant (a brick can be said to *lie* or to *stand* on the table, which makes a difference as to its position, but there is no sense to say of a brick that it is standing *upside down*). In short, the categorization shown in Fig. 8 reflects, to a certain extent, the conditions encoded in the lexical meaning of *to lie, to stand, to turn upside down* etc. This confirms the claim made at the beginning, and provides further evidence in support of the assignment types discussed in (28)-(32) above.

Fourth, the DAP ACROSS, as will be remembered, is in any case assigned a contextually induced value (cf. the remarks in Fn. 7). Due to the fact, however, that ACROSS is a stop-gap of **IPS** and **PPS**, it is neutral with respect to mobility features and hence applies across movable and immobile objects (as indicated by ▦ dotted backgrounding in Fig. 8).

Fifth, Fig. 8 offers a complete categorization of objects with respect to intrinsically or/and deictically assigned sides. This information is accessed in the interpretation of projective prepositions such as *above - below* and/or *in front of - behind* (for details see Lang (1990b)). The overlapping area marked by ▨ at the bottom of Fig. 8 shows the range of objects that are available for both intrinsic and deictic assignment of sides.

Fig. 8 The Interaction of Dimension, Position, and Side-based Region Assignment to Spatial Objects

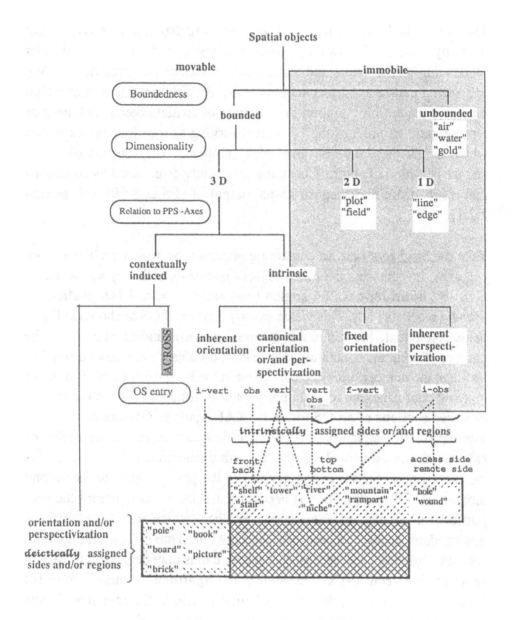

2.3   Object Schemata (OS)

2.3.1   The Make-up of OS

The most suitable way to represent concepts of spatial objects is to represent them by means of a **matrix with 3 rows** and **1, 2, or 3 columns** (depending on the nature and number of the axes of the given object). We call such a matrix an **object schema** (OS). An OS contains entries which represent the defining properties of a class of spatial objects. OS are thus representational units of the CS - level serving as location frames within which the DAPs of the SF - level are instantiated. The structure of an OS and the selection of entries it contains are entirely determined by conditions that result from the categorizational output of **IPS** and **PPS** (cf. section 2.2.1).

Take the head row first. In containing one, two, or three variables for object axes, it represents the given object's **dimensionality** by a, a b, or a b c, **boundedness** by angled brackets < ... >, and **integration of axes** by brackets (...). This yields exactly 7 types of OS as shown in Fig. 9 below. Note that, due to possible integration of axes indicated by (...), the number of columns containing information on object axes may be equal or less than the number of object axes given in the head row of an OS. In order to avoid confusion, the relevant portions of information (i.e. columns) will be called **sections of an OS** (or, in OSKAR's jargon, OS-sections).
The alphabetic sequence 'a – b – c' is meant to reflect the **order of salience** of the axes involved, that is, with disintegrated object axes, 'a' is the place-holder for the maximal axis, 'b' the place-holder for the second longest, etc. This stipulation is necessary and useful to represent the proportions of an object's axes to one another, which may vary partially independent of their dimensional assignment. Thus, within the general concept "building", the vertically designated axis may decreasingly vary in salience between (a)"sky-scraper", (b)"apartment house", and (c) "bungalow". Similarly, the ratio of height to width differentiates objects within the class of receptacles (cf. "barrel" vs. "saucepan").

The convention at issue thus accounts for **proportional variations** that may occur within a class of objects that are alike as to their dimensional assignments but differ in their proportions.

The second row of an OS reflects defining gestalt and position properties of the given object, that is, it contains **primary entries** such as max, sub, dist, vert, obs, flach. Being part of an OS, these symbols now stand for **DAVs** (Dimension Assignment Values) which instantiate the DAPs (Dimension Assignment Parameters) MAX, SUB, VERT etc. of the SF - level. The typographic distinction (Times CAPS vs. Courier small letters) is used to indicate the difference between semantic and conceptual elements. Making use of the same labels for elements of both sets signifies the correspondence of DAPs and DAVs with respect to gestalt and position properties of objects. Entries contained in the second row of an OS are conceived as primary entries which instantiate the pertinent DAP by way of **identification**. This is formally expressed by matching entries in the second and third row of an OS-section (cf. (34)(a)).

The third row displays the conceptual effects as produced by the instantiation of a DAP or by the situational context. This is the place where all the non-intrinsic dimension and position assignments (shown in the left hand side of Fig. 8) are spelled out explicitly. The formal operation accounting for this is called **contextual specification**. What it amounts to is that a certain DAV is inserted into the third row of an OS-section.

The conditions according to which entries in the second and third row of an OS-section may differ are determined by a set of COMPATIBILITY CONDITIONS. These conditions define the range of admissible assignments based on which a given object axis, predetermined by primary entries concerning gestalt and/or position properties, can be specified with respect to its **actual reference to the surrounding space**.

To give just one simple example, consider the two OS representing the semantic interpretation of *the pole* in (34)(a) and (b):

(34)(a)   The pole is 10m long   <   a   (b   c) >
                                           max   sub
                                           max

(b)   The pole is 10m high   <   a   (b   c) >
                                       max   sub
                                       vert

Primary identification, as will be recalled, is represented by matching entries in the second and third row. The combination [max max] in (34)(a) thus indicates that the DAdj *long* identifies the maximal axis of the pole. **Contextually induced specification**, however, is represented by differing but compatible entries in the second and third row. Hence the combination [max vert] in (34)(b) indicates that the DAdj *high* applies to the pole's maximal axis by specifying it as coincident with the Vertical of **PPS**. In other words, *high* specifies the pole's actual reference to the surrounding space. (34)(b) entails that the pole is standing, whereas (34)(a) is unspecified as to the pole's position. Now, contrast this with (35)(a,b), where *pole* is replaced with *tower*, which has a slightly different OS:

(35)(a)   The tower is 10m high/tall   <   a   (b   c)>
                                                max   sub
                                                <u>vert</u>
                                                vert

    (b)   *The tower is 10m long   <   a   (b   c)>
                                                max   sub
                                                <u>vert</u>
                                                ???

Note that the first OS-section of the OS for *tower* contains, as one complex primary entry, what in the case of *pole* in (34)(b) is the combinatorial result of contextual specification. The complex entry [max vert] in the OS "tower" indicates (i) that a tower has a canonical orientation regarding verticality (symbolized by the entry vert in the second row); and (ii) that the canonical verticality feature is bound to the tower's maximal axis.

Given this, the device that maps DAPs onto OS is designed in such a way that the following holds: the complex entry [max vert] in the OS of *tower* is accessible to the DAP VERT encoded in the meaning of *high* or *tall*, that is, VERT can be instantiated as vert by way of **identification**, cf. (35)(a). The entry [max vert] is, however, not accessible to MAX (or any other DAP). In such cases, MAX cannot be instantiated by way of identification (the component max of the complex entry cannot be addressed separately), nor can MAX be instantiated by way of specification. Specification of **PPS**-determined DAVs by **IPS**-parameters is excluded on principled grounds: gestalt properties of objects may be specified as position properties, but not *vice versa* - cf. Lang 1989:Chap. 3.

As indicated by '???', the sentence (35)(b) *The tower is 10m long* does not have a regular interpretation, that is, one that would meet the conditions set by CANONICAL ORIENTATION. This is the first thing the theory (and correspondingly, OSKAR) has to say about cases like (35)(b). In addition to that, however, it does provide an interpretation of (35)(b) to the extent that the object at issue has to be conceived as having lost its canonical position due to positional changes (e.g. by toppling down). The formal device to account for this **marked interpretation** of (35)(b) is a procedure which removes the component `vert` from the complex entry [`max vert`]. The removal of canonical assignments, thus effected, paves the way for the DAP MAX to be instantiated in a modified OS for *tower*. This is the way **OSKAR** deals with (all admissible sorts of) positional variation of movable objects. See the details in sections 3.3.1 - 3.3.3.

Before discussing the COMPATIBILITY CONDITIONS that constrain the admissible combinations of DAVs in an OS, we should have a look at two illustrative samples of OS, just to form an idea of their internal make-up.

(36) (a) "wall"   < a   b   c   >
                        max   vert   sub

   (b) "Great Wall"   < a   b   c   >
       (of China)   max   vert   across

   (c) "ruler"   < a   b   c   >
                        max   ivert   sub

   (d) "river"   < a   b   c   >
                        max   across   vert
                                         obs

(37) (a) "wound"   < a   b   c   >
                          ∅   ∅   iobs

   (b) "brick"   < a   b   c   >
                          ∅   ∅   sub

An examination of the four OS in (36) will reveal the characteristic spatial features that either group together or distinguish the objects thus represented.

First, note the minimal but crucial differences among the top three OS. From the point of view of dimensional designation, a wall and a ruler comprise the same set of DAVs (both have length, height and thickness), but whereas a wall has a feature for canonical verticality, a ruler has one for inherent verticality. The former is represented in the OS by the (non-prefixed) primary entry `vert`, the latter by the prefixed entry `ivert`. The entry `f-vert` accounts for the immobility of e.g. "hill" - see Fig. 8. This suffices to establish the distinct position and mobility properties of these objects, see the discussion in section 2.2.3 above.

Second, note the occurrences of the DAV `across` in (36) (b) and (d). As will be remembered, it is due to the inherent relativity of the DAP ACROSS (underlying the interpretation of *breit* or *wide*, cf. Fn. 7) that the corresponding DAV `across` is bound to context-dependent instantiations. This applies also to the internal structure of OS. The canonical entries `vert` and [vert obs] in the OS for "Great Wall" and "river", respectively, provide the necessary OS-internal context information for appropriately narrowing down the slot to be filled with `across`. This then neatly reflects one of the differences between the objects in (36)(b) and (d) and those exemplified in (37)(a, b). Objects like "brick" or "wound" allow for a wider range of possible instantiations of `across` and therefore contain the empty entry ø in the relevant OS-sections.

Third, one should take notice of the significant difference in depth assignment as represented by the OS for "river" and "wound", respectively. The complex entry [vert obs] indicates the alignment of an object's axis to the Vertical and the Observer Axis in such a way that they run parallel but in diametrically opposed directions - cf. (28)(2) above. The entry `iobs` in the OS for "wound", however, marks INHERENT PERSPECTIVIZATION as discussed in (32)(b) - cf. section 2.2.3 above. The difference between the entries [vert obs] and `iobs` is sufficient to account for the different position and mobility characteristics of the objects in question. Cf. the places of "wound" and "river" in the taxonomy shown in Fig. 8.

So much for the internal structure of OS. As has been mentioned above, the OS are a means to represent object concepts, that is, they are designed to reflect those basic gestalt and position properties that determine the conceptualization of objects as carriers of spatial characteristics along the lines sketched right at the beginning of the present paper.

From a theoretical point of view, the most interesting finding appears to be this:

(38) <u>Both</u> the full range of possible object schemata <u>and</u> the scope of admissible dimensional designations and positional variations of objects can be shown to be completely determined by a small set of COMPATIBILITY CONDITIONS.

We will take a brief look at them in the next section.

2.3.2   Compatibility Conditions Underlying the Assignment of Dimensions and Positions to Objects in Space

Referring to the groups of facts mentioned in (10) - (15), (18) - (20), (25) - (26) and drawing together various threads of argument concerning **IPS** and **PPS** as well as the different types of ORIENTATION and PERSPECTIVIZATION of objects (recall subsections 2.2.1 - 2.2.3 above), we may come up with the following general statements:

(39) (a) An object schema OS is an n - tuple of OS-sections each of which may contain a limited set of entries representing Dimension Assignment Values (DAVs).

   (b) The set of basic elements occurring as entries in OS to represent DAVs can reasonably be restricted to the following set
        B = { max, obs, vert, sub, dist, across, ø }

   (c) The combination and distribution of the elements of **B** within an OS is determined by a set of conceptually motivated COMPATIBILITY CONDITIONS, which include the following selection:

(40) (1) max, sub, dist, ø are always the first entry in an OS-section
      (2) sub, across, obs are always the last entry in an OS-section
      (3) If an OS contains an entry obs, then this OS may not contain an entry sub , and *vice versa*.
      (4) Each element **b** from **B**, **b** ≠ ø, occurs at most once in an OS, and ø never occurs alone etc.

The complete set of the COMPATIBILITY CONDITIONS (comprising a total of 12 conditions to cope with all possible OS) is discussed in the Epilogue to Bierwisch/Lang 1987, 1989 and need not be presented here in detail. What is worth being looked at more closely, however, is the results emerging from these constraints. Based on the COMPATIBILITY CONDITIONS as illustrated by (40)(1) - (4), the set of admissible (simple and complex) entries that may occur in an OS-section is restricted to the following set (we neglect the prefixed variants of vert and obs):

(41)   max,   vert,   obs,   across, sub,   dist,   ∅,

         vert ,   max ,   max ,   ∅   ,   ∅   ,   ∅
         obs   vert   obs   across   vert   obs

The list of admissible entries representing possible Dimension Assignment Values in OS-sections reflects in a sufficiently abstract way the conceptual structure of the cognitive submodule C_{SPACE} which is responsible for dimensional designation and positional variation of objects, and hence, for the pertinent categorization of objects in space.

The nicest generalization captured by (41) is this: the list of possible complex entries given in the second row mirrors the compatibility of gestalt and position properties (as defined by **IPS** and **PPS**) as such. That means that the COMPATIBILITY CONDITIONS define a combination like [max vert] or [vert obs] as an **admissible combination** of spatial properties to be assigned to an object. This definition is valid independent of the way the complex entry happens to come about and therefore also independent of the distinction between intrinsic and contextually induced assignments.

    For instance, the basic admissibility of the combination [max vert] lays the ground for having the corresponding complex entry as a primary entry in an OS (as with "tower" in (35)(a)) or for having it as the outcome of contextually induced specification (as with the OS for *high pole* in (34)(b)). What is more, the list of admissible combinations given in (41) is also the conceptual basis from which possible semantic encodings of Dimension Assignment Parameters at the lexical level can be predicted. Thus, (41) represents a list of admissible parameter combinations from which the particular languages take their lexical options.

To give just one example: the Semantic Form of the English DAdj *tall* exactly picks out the conjunction of MAX & VERT, that is, it covers a combination of DAPs that is licensed by the COMPATIBILITY CONDITIONS. Thus, in view of the validity of (41), the meaning structure of *tall* is within the scope of predictable semantic combinations, whereas the lexical coverage of this combination remains open to language-particular variation (e.g. German lacks an equivalent to *tall*). The prediction to be made is this: though there is some variation among languages as to the lexical structure of dimensional expressions, it should be highly improbable to find a language having a dimension expression which covers incompatible Dimension Assignment Parameters, say SUB & DIST or OBS & SUB. In sum, (41) leaves us with the suggestion of a working hypothesis on linguistic universals, which reads:

(42)   The possible semantic structure of dimension expressions is universally constrained by the COMPATIBILITY CONDITIONS but cross-linguistically open to varying lexicalization

After this look at the very fundamentals of the conceptualization of space, we will now turn to their manifestation in our conceptual repertoire.

2.3.3   The Inventory of OS

The inventory of those admissible object schemata for which we were able to find some empirical instances is presented in Fig. 9 (and continued in Fig. 9') below. Well, we would not argue about adding one or two further OS that might have escaped us. But if this is granted, we may claim that the catalogue of OS presented below is **exhaustive** as regards the distribution and combination of spatial properties involved in dimensional designation and positional variation of objects.

To round off the insights to be gained from the conceptual categorization that underlies the inventory of OS, we will add a few comments after the illustration. Objects with three disintegrated axes obviously allow for the widest range of variation regarding DAVs in their OS, thus the enumeration of the distinct OS of type IV is continued in Fig. 9' below.

Fig. 9   Categorization of Spatial Objects at the Conceptual Level
and Inventory of Object Schemata

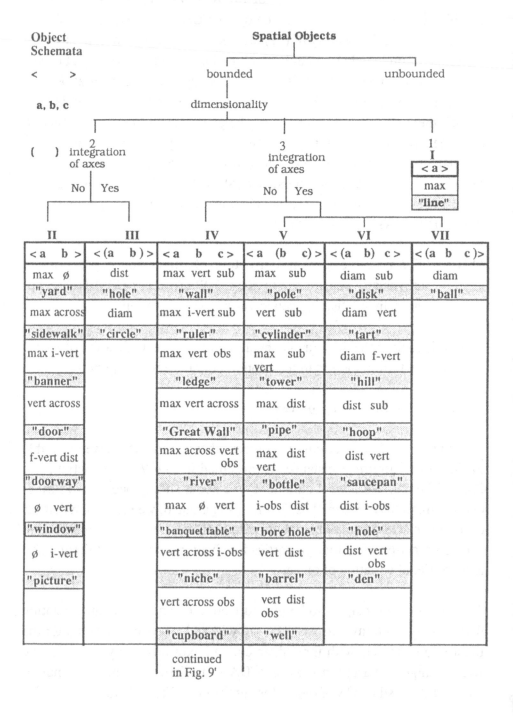

Fig. 9 ' Further OS of Type IV

IV

< a	b	c >
max	across	vert
i-obs		
"mine hole"		
across	obs	vert
"stair"		
max	ø	ø
vert		
obs		
"elevator shaft"		
i-vert	ø	sub
"book"		
ø	vert	obs
"chest"		
obs	dist	vert
"doorway"		
ø	ø	sub
"brick"		
ø	ø	i-obs
"wound"		
ø	ø	vert
"coffin"		

Construed as a conceptual memory stock, each of the OS shown above represents a selected configuration of gestalt and/or position properties of a class of spatial objects. Note that within this framework, the notion "class of objects" is strictly defined in terms of OS, not in terms of similarity of shape or function. Thus 'class membership' here means 'sharing the same OS', and in this sense "tree", "tower", "pillar", "mast" etc. belong to one and the same class. In other words, each of the 45 Object Schemata shown in Fig. 9 covers a collection of objects which would not be grouped together from a functional or geometrical point of view.

In taxonomic terms, an OS is a blend of features of diverse origin and structure. The basic features are those provided by the PRINCIPLES OF OBJECT DELIMITATION - cf. (27). They define the seven **types of OS** (**I - VII** in Fig. 9) which, in turn, are filled with entries that are determined by the **IPS** categorization grid. The latter, in turn, have a basis differing from that of the **PPS**-determined entries. It is precisely in this sense that an OS represents a conceptually designated intersection range of heterogeneous categorizations which is stored as a concept in long-term memory due to its relevance for human behaviour in a spatial environment.

From this, two conclusions are to be drawn: (1) The typology of object concepts shown in Fig. 9 must be seen as self-contained and not reducible to other categorizations. (2) The gestalt and position properties of objects reflected in the OS provide the natural basis for functional parameters according to which objects are evaluated with respect to pragmatic purposes. It is the latter which are projected onto the former, not the other way round. So much for the ontological status of OS[15].

Finally, a few remarks on the interaction of constraints that narrow down the set of admissible OS to the inventory shown in Fig. 9. On sheer perusal, one will observe that, given the types I - VII, the next strongest restriction after boundedness and dimensionality is exerted by axial integration. Objects having only integrated axes (III and VII) are practically confined to one DAV. Even where only two of three axes are integrated (V and VI), the range of possible combinations and distributions of DAVs in OS is heavily restricted. Not surprisingly, then, only the class of objects with three disintegrated axes (IV) displays the full range of value configurations

---

[15]   An interesting proposal towards a deeper understanding of the structure of domain-specific knowledge as codified in OS has been put forth by Blutner (in press).

allowed for by the COMPATIBILITY CONDITIONS.

Given the principles illustrated in Figures 7, 8, and 9, the reader has the means to gain a comprehensive insight into the highly abstract but efficient elements and conditions organizing the cognitive submodule C$_{SPACE}$, which is responsible for dimensional designation and positional variation of objects in space. And it is, by no means accidentally, these principles that form the essential procedural building blocks of the Prolog program OSKAR, cf. sections 3.3 and 3.4 below.

2.3.4   Intrinsic and Deictic Sides

In the course of implementing the theory discussed so far, the notion of object schema underwent some further elaboration. Having specified in the OS the pertinent object axes for ORIENTATION and PERSPECTIVIZATION, the idea to use the very same informational source for the assignment of intrinsic and deictic sides to objects suggested itself.

Drawing on the information available in an OS like (35) - (37), the assigment of axis-determined sides can be carried out in the following way. Recall that the object axes **a, b, c** represented by the OS-sections are conceived as segments with respective pairs of endpoints, say A1, A2; B1, B2; C1, C3. Now, based on the fact that the relevant object axes are orthogonal to one another, the endpoints A1, A2 of object axis **a** will be perpendicular to an object side s which is formed by **b** x **c**, and likewise with the endpoints B1, B2 etc.

Given this, we are enabled to identify the six different sides of a three-dimensional object with disintegrated axes without further ado. Now, the interesting point is how this device can be used to exploit the information on verticality and perspective as contained in the OS, that is, the entries vert and obs. The device is as simple as it is efficient. Take the following OS, which, in a nutshell, contains all the entries needed for assigning **intrinsic sides** to an object.

(43)   "cupboard"   <a   b   c   >
                        vert   across   obs
                        F´, i_os   S, i_lis   O´, i_rs
                        F , i_us   S´,i_res   O , i_vs
                        ─────────────────────────────────────

The head row and the second row of the OS remain as before but are now furnished with additional entries for endpoints and endpoint-related sides, respectively. Thus, the endpoints F, F' of the canonically oriented vertical axis of a cupboard now serve to assign to that cupboard an intrinsic **bottom side** (i_us, German: *Unterseite*) and an intrinsic **top side** (i_os, German: *Oberseite*), respectively.

Similarly, the endpoints O, O' of the canonically perspectivized depth axis of a cupboard are used to determine the object's intrinsic **front side** (i_vs, German: *Vorderseite*) and **rear side** (i_rs, German: *Rückseite*), respectively. The endpoints of the third axis, which by themselves would not have designated values due to the specific nature of across, are - in the given context of the other OS-sections - marked as carriers of intrinsic **lefthand side** (i_lis) and **righthand side** (i_res), respectively.

It should be evident that the addition to OS-sections of entries for intrinsic sides provides us with a highly welcome completion of the spatial information represented in an OS.

Analoguously, the assignment of **deictic top** and **bottom** and **front** and **rear sides** proceeds along the lines sketched above, with the only difference that the assignment of deictic sides is bound to DAVs that enter an OS via contextually induced specification. This is treated in more detail in the subsections of section 3.3 below.

Once we have information on intrinsically and deictically assigned object sides at our disposal, we are able to come to grips with a wider range of facts about spatial relations. Among them the various ways in which objects are localized with respect to one another (*x is in front of y*, *x is below y* , *x lies on y* etc.) and, above all, the full range of positional changes a given object may undergo. How OSKAR manages to deal with the latter complex of phenomena will be shown in section 3.3.

Having discussed the DAPs in section 2.2 and the OS in section 2.3, we are left with the discussion of the third component of the theory. As the two constituent parts have been presented in sufficient detail, we may now be brief in sketching the device which determines their interaction.

2.4   Dimensional Designation = mapping DAPs onto OS

2.4.1   Identification vs. Specification.

To recapitulate, we may put it like this: in formal terms, the semantics of dimensional designations is a mapping device which takes a pair (OS, DAP) as its argument and maps it onto an appropriate range of values DAV, where OS is an object schema, DAP is a Dimension Assigment Parameter, and DAV is a set of Dimension Assigment Values forming entries in an OS-section such that DAV is either **identified** or **specified** by the DAP in question.

Having established that, all we have to do is give some details on the specific structure of this mapping, that is, on the elements that occur in the domain and range, and also on the two basic operations called **identification** and **specification** of a DAP with respect to a DAV.

(44)   The set of Dimension Assignment Parameters at issue is given by
         DAP={ MAX, SUB, DIST, VERT, OBS, ACROSS, FLACH, SIZE }

Now, a Dimension Assigment Parameter P is mapped onto a DAV p by way of Identification iff P matches with p according to the typographic convention introduced in 2.3.1 above. Neglecting the DAP SIZE, we get:

(45)   **Identification:** $P \Rightarrow p$,
         where $P \in$ { MAX, SUB, DIST, VERT, OBS, ACROSS, FLACH },
                  $p \in$ {max, sub, dist, vert, obs } and
                  p is the last entry in an OS-section.

In contrast, a Dimension Assignment Parameter Q is mapped onto a DAV p by way of Specification iff Q attaches a DAV q to the DAV p in an OS-section. Attachment is restricted by suitable conditions determining possible specifications. Somewhat simplified, we get the following:

(46)   **Specification:** $Q \Rightarrow p$,
         where $Q \in$ { VERT, OBS, ACROSS, FLACH },
                  $p \in$ { max, ø, vert } and
                  p is licensed as a landing site for Q in OS

The constraints on possible specification follow from the COMPATIBILITY CONDITIONS discussed in section 2.3.2 above. For details, ask OSKAR.

2.4.2   Inferences

Recall the types of inferences shown in (20) above, e.g. that *the pole is 3m high* entails *the pole is 3m long*, whereas *the wall is 3m high* does not entail *the wall is 3m long*. What the theory provides as a solution to this problem now appears to be merely a by-product of (46). In fact, these inferences are neatly accounted for by reversing (46), that is, by an operation of **de-specification.** The class of entailments in question can be shown to be valid by carrying out the procedure of **de-specification** on contextually specified OS. The application of this procedure is governed by two simple rules, which in terms of (45) and (46) read thus:

(47)   **De-specification:**

(R1)   For any OS for object x with an OS-section entry [p I q], there is an OS' for x with an OS-section entry [p I p].

(R2)   For any OS for object x with an OS-section entry [ø I q], there is an OS' for x with an OS-section entry [ø I across].

So ultimately it is just the two mapping operations (45) and (46) which account for the whole range of seemingly complicated facts about dimensional designation of objects in space.

The prerequisite for coming to results as simple and clear-cut as these seems to be: a modular approach to cognition which links meticulous examination of linguistic data with careful theorizing on the abstract principles that might explain their underlying regularities.

The fact that the theory of dimensional designation developed along these lines could be implemented in Prolog rather straightforwardly may well be taken as additional confirmation of this approach. So it's time to get acquainted with OSKAR. We will introduce the program in steps that roughly correspond to the subsections of the present chapter.

3. The Implementation of OSKAR

3.0 Introductory Remarks

In 1988, we began implementing the theory of dimensional designation as outlined in the previous sections. The result is the Prolog program OSKAR. Originally, the implementation was meant to be a means for testing the formal apparatus of the theory as to its **consistency** (no incorrect designations) and **completeness** (exhaustive applicability on spatial objects). To that end, both the theory and the program proved to be successful, which certainly is a welcome result in its own right. But what is more, in the course of developing OSKAR (by 'rapid prototyping') we were faced with some aspects of spatial knowledge which had not been taken into consideration before. These are, above all, rules and principles determining side assignment and positional variation. Moreover, they could be analyzed and integrated into the program very easily. Thus encouraged, we will present in this section the logical structure and the conceptual substance of OSKAR in some detail.

3.1 Outline of the Structure of OSKAR

As a first approximation, the structure of OSKAR comprises the following components:

(a) Transformation of natural language Input into its semantic content (DAPs and OS) and
(b) Interpretation of the DAPs with respect to the OS and display of the result as Output (see Fig. 10 below).

The Input to OSKAR can be any combination of an object name and one or more DAdjs, the latter being used either in attributive (*high tower, long and thick pole*) and/or predicative use (*Is a tower high?, A thick pole is long*). This natural language Input is transformed into intermediate structures in which adjectives and nouns are replaced by appropriately retrieved DAPs and OS, respectively. These structures, in turn, form the Input to the interpretation component of OSKAR, which is discussed in detail in section 3.3 below. Notice that this way of proceeding allows us to abstract from syntax, parsing and semantic construction and also from the gradation aspects of dimensional adjectives mentioned in section 2.1.3.

Fig. 10   The Components of OSKAR in Outline

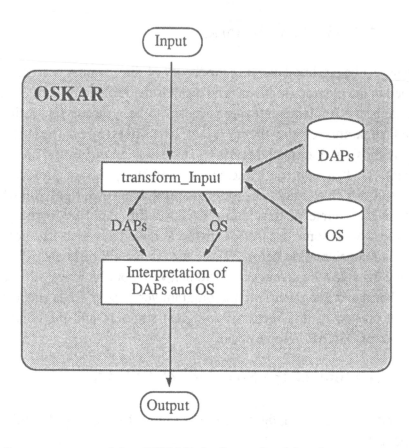

The <u>Output</u> generated by OSKAR is determined by the success or the failure of the interpretation of the DAPs and the OS. In case of success, the actual dimensional assignments of the (possibly updated) OS and the object's current position properties are shown. Otherwise, an appropriate error message is delivered.

This simplified overall structure of OSKAR is reflected in the Prolog code shown in (48):

```
(48)   oskar:-
          repeat,
          transform_input_to_DAPs_and_OS(DAPs_and_OS),
          interpretation_of_DAPs_and_OS(DAPs_and_OS),
          fail.

       transform_input_to_DAPs_and_OS(DAPs_and_OS):-
          get_input(Input),
          transform_input_to_DAPs_and_OS(Input,DAPs_and_OS),!.
       interpretation_of_DAPs_and_OS(DAPs_and_OS):-
          interpretation_of_DAPs_and_OS(DAPs_and_OS,Message),
          put_output(Message), !.
```

3.2   The Representation of DAPs and OS in OSKAR

Dimensional Assignment Parameters (DAPs). To capture the distinction between the <u>semantic</u> DAPs and the <u>conceptual</u> DAVs (cf. section 2.2), they are represented as CAPITALIZED and non-capitalized Prolog atoms, respectively. The correlations between adjectives, DAPs and DAVs is shown in the following table.

adjective(s)	DAP	DAV(s)
langl kurz	`'MAX'`	`max, imax`
breitl schmal	`'ACROSS'`	`across`
dickl dünn	`'SUB'`	`sub/d_sub`
weitl eng	`'DIST'`	`dist/d_dist`
flach	`'FLACH'`	`flach`
hochl niedrig	`'VERT'`	`vert, ivert`
tief	`'OBS'`	`obs, iobs`
grossl klein	`'SIZE'`	`('*')`
-	-	`diam`
-	-	`empty`

`imax`, `ivert`, and `iobs` are the DAVs representing inherent length, orientation and perspectivization, respectively. In contrast to `sub` and `dist`, which represent qualities of integrated axes, `d_sub` and `d_dist` were introduced to model the same qualities, but with respect to disintegrated axes. `empty` is simply OSKAR's version of the symbol ⌀.[16]

Object schemata (OS) - cf. section 2.3 - are represented in OSKAR as feature structures implemented as complex Prolog terms. A feature therefore has the form ATTRIBUTE(VALUE), where VALUE can be a complex structure (i.e. a list of features or a list of special values represented in turn as Prolog terms) or an atom.

---

16   There is more to the interpretation of this DAV than, for example, "an axis without any assignments". Note that it must be a disintegrated axis to allow for the contextual specification by 'VERT', 'OBS' or 'ACROSS'. To regard `empty` as a landing site for these DAPs, which, on the other hand, has to be present after de-specification of the pertinent contextually specified DAVs, was one of the ideas which emerged with the development of procedures for positional change of objects. This view of `empty` opened the way for modelling immobility of objects (see section 3.5.1).

```
(49)              os([    dimensions(DIMENSIONS),
                         sections(SECTIONS),
                         nop(NOP),
                         sides(SIDES) ] )
```

```
(50)      section([  axes(AXES),
                     boundedness(BOUNDEDNESS),
                     endpoints(ENDPOINTS),
                     assignment(DAVs)  ])
```

(49) illustrates the general form of an object schema in OSKAR. It contains the information discussed in section 2.3.1 about an object's

- dimensionality (DIMENSIONS)
- OS-sections (SECTIONS)
- normal proportion (NOP) and sides (SIDES).

Currently, the attribute 'nop' is merely a dummy whose range still must be fixed.[17]

(50) illustrates the general form of an OS-section in an object schema OS. It contains the following information:

- the involved axes (AXES)
- the boundedness wrt. the OS-section (BOUNDEDNESS)
- the endpoints of the OS-section (ENDPOINTS) and
- the dimension assignment values (DAVs)

Since AXES is always a subset of DIMENSIONS, the unique identification of an OS-section is guaranteed. The explicit notation of the endpoints of an axis has two advantageous consequences:

- It provides the representation of OS with the means for distinguishing among the directions an axis may assume. This is especially important for representing an object axis' alignment to the Vertical or to the Observer axis. For this reason, DAVs are represented as two-place terms whose arguments represent the endpoints of the axis in question (e.g. vert(a1,a2)).

---

[17]   ´nop´ stands for the standard proportion of objects and is indispensable for an adequate treatment of *groß - klein*, or *big - small* (see Lang 1989: Chap.5).

- It enables us to assign intrinsic and deictic (i.e. contextually induced) sides to the object (cf. section 2.3.3). Thus we can model the 'sidedness' of objects (cf. Miller/Johnson-Laird 1976). This is done in OSKAR by introducing terms of the type s(ENDPOINT,I,D) as components of SIDES, where I and D are variables which may be instantiated by constants representing intrinsic and deictic sides, respectively.

(51) and (52) show the OS of "pole" and "tower" as represented in OSKAR. The slight but crucial difference of the OS rests on the canonical position of a tower: the OS of "tower" has a vert entry and intrinsic top and bottom side while the OS of "pole" does not.

(51) "pole":

```
os([ dimensions([a,b,c]),
     sections([  section([  axes([a]),
                            boundedness(bounded),
                            endpoints([a1,a2]),
                            assignment([max(a1,a2)])]),
                                          /* length/height */
                 section([  axes([b,c]),
                            boundedness(bounded),
                            endpoints([d1,d2]),
                            assignment([sub(d1,d2)])])]),
                                          /* thickness */
     nop('*'),
     sides([ s(a1,_,_), s(a2,_,_),s(d1,_,_),s(d2,_,_)]) ])
```

(52) "tower":

```
os([ dimensions([a,b,c]),
     sections([  section([  axes([a]),
                            boundedness(bounded),
                            endpoints([a1,a2]),
                            assignment([max(a1,a2),vert(a1,a2)])]),
                                          /* height */
                 section([  axes([b,c]),
                            boundedness(bounded),
                            endpoints([d1,d2]),
                            assignment([sub(d1,d2)])])]),
                                          /* thickness */
     nop('*'),
     sides([ s(a1,i_us,_), s(a2,i_os,_),s(d1,_,_),s(d2,_,_)]) ])
```

(53) and (54) show examples for objects with inherent orientation (ivert) or perspectivization (iobs) (cf. section 2.2.3), (55) gives an example of an object without any characteristic reference to the surrounding space.

(53) "book"

```
os([ dimensions([a,b,c]),
     sections([ section([ axes([a]),
                          boundedness(bounded),
                          endpoints([a1,a2]),
                          assignment([ivert(a1,a2)])]),
                section([ axes([b]),
                          boundedness(bounded),
                          endpoints([b1,b2]),
                          assignment([empty(b1,b2)])]),
                section([ axes([c]),
                          boundedness(bounded),
                          endpoints([c1,c2])]),
                          assignment([sub(c1,c2)])])]),
     nop('*'),
     sides([ s(a1,i_us,_),s(a2,i_os,_),s(b1,i_lis,_),s(b2,i_res,_),
             s(c1,i_vs,_),s(c2,i_rs,_)])
     ]))
```

(54) "hole"

```
os([ dimensions([a,b,c]),
     sections([ section([ axes([a,b]),
                          boundedness(bounded),
                          endpoints([d1,d2]),
                          assignment([dist(d1,d2)])]),
                section([ axes([c]),
                          boundedness(bounded),
                          endpoints([c1,c2]),
                          assignment([iobs(c1,c2)])])]),
     nop('*'),
     sides([ s(d1,_,_),s(d2,_,_),s(c1,i_vs,_),s(c2,_,_)])
     ])).
```

(55) "brick"

```
os([ dimensions([a,b,c]),
     sections([ section([ axes([a]),
                          boundedness(bounded),
                          endpoints([a1,a2]),
                          assignment([empty(a1,a2)])]),
                section([ axes([b]),
                          boundedness(bounded),
                          endpoints([b1,b2]),
                          assignment([empty(b1,b2)])]),
                section([ axes([c]),
                          boundedness(bounded),
                          endpoints([c1,c2])]),
                          assignment([sub(c1,c2)])])]),
     nop('*'),
     sides([ s(a1,_,_),s(a2,_,_),s(b1,_,_),s(b2,_,_),
             s(c1,_,_),s(c2,_,_)])
     ]))
```

The PROPORTION of an object, i.e. the order of the sections within an OS according to the prominence of the corresponding axes, is reflected in the order of the elements of the lists instantiating the VALUE of `sections`. INTEGRATEDNESS of object axes is not expressed directly in the OS but it can be inferred from the number of axes of the respective OS-section.

BASIC SCHEMATA - as a means for modelling the variations within a family of OS - and their specialization to OS like (51) - (55) are not implemented in OSKAR (instead one object class may simply be assigned more than one object schema). Yet we are convinced that this aspect can be integrated very easily into any flexible knowledge representation system (see Fn. 38).

3.3 The Interaction of DAPs and OS

3.3.1 Assigning Dimensions and Positions to Objects

The INTERPRETATION of the DAPs and the OS extracted from a given Input takes place as a successive EVALUATION of single DAPs with respect to the OS. Such an EVALUATION of a DAP can be roughly described as the application of rules for IDENTIFICATION and SPECIFICATION to some DAV in the OS, while simultaneously checking the COMPATIBILITY CONDITIONS specified by the theory of dimensional designation (cf. section 2.3.2). Three kinds of rules evaluating a DAP are distinguished:

R1 : identification of a DAV
R2 : gestalt specification of a DAV
R3 : contextually induced specification of a DAV

Regarding IDENTIFICATION and SPECIFICATION, these rules can be cross-classified in the following manner: on the one hand, R2 and R3 are specification rules in that they restrict the possible dimensional or positional interpretations of the object in question. Both rules lead to a new, 'specified' object schema OS´ in which the DAV corresponding to the DAP has been inserted into the `assignment` of the pertinent OS-section. On the other hand, R1 and R2 can be understood as simply identifying an object axis without affecting any position of the object. This is reflected in the following `eval_DAP` procedure of OSKAR:

(56)

```
eval_DAP(DAP,OS,OSNEW,P_NUM,ident):-
    identify_DAV(DAP,OS,OSNEW,OldAssign,NewAssign,P_NUM).

eval_DAP(DAP,OS,OSNEW,P_NUM,ident):-
    gestaltspecify_DAV(DAP,OS,OS1,OldAssign,NewAssign,P_NUM),
    change_and_copy([sections, section, assignment],
                    OS1,OldAssig,NewAssign,OSNEW).

eval_DAP(DAP,OS,OSNEW,P_NUM,spec):-
    contextually_specify_DAV(DAP,OS,OS1,
                                  OldAssign,NewAssign,P_NUM),
    change_and_copy([sections, section, assignment],
                    OS1,OldAssign,NewAssign,OSNEW).
```

We will now elaborate the three relevant subprocedures of `eval_DAP` with some illustrative examples. This will clarify their Prolog realization in OSKAR, shown in (57) below.

The IDENTIFICATION of a DAV with respect to a DAP can be described as follows: The last entries in the `assignments` of the OS are looked up in order to find a DAV matching with the DAP. To give an example, the DAV `vert` in the OS of "tower" (see (52)) matches with the DAP `'VERT'` of *high* . In case of success, the appropriate assignment of deictic sides is carried out. For our example *high tower*, this results in the following instantiation of the sides component:

```
sides([s(a1,i_us,d_us),s(a2,i_os,d_os),s(d1,_,_),s(d2,_,_)])])
```

We see that the intrinsic and deictic top and bottom sides coincide as should be the case with canonically oriented objects in normal position.

Similarly, the GESTALTSPECIFICATION of a DAV begins with the search for an entry in the OS which is accessible for gestalt specification and at the same time meets the overall restrictions on gestalt specification (cf. section 2.3.1). For *the brick is long and wide* this means that the evaluation of the DAPs `'MAX'` and `'ACROSS'` results in the insertion of the DAVs `max` and `across` in the first and second section of the OS of "brick", respectively. Cf. (55) modified here as (55'):

(55') "brick"

```
os([  dimensions([a,b,c]),
      sections([  section([ axes([a]),
                            boundedness(bounded),
                            endpoints([a1,a2]),
                            assignment([empty(a1,a2),max(a1,a2)])]),
                  section([ axes([b]),
                            boundedness(bounded),
                            endpoints([b1,b2]),
                            assignment([empty(b1,b2),across(b1,b2)])]),
                  section([ axes([c]),
                            boundedness(bounded),
                            endpoints([c1,c2])]),
                            assignment([sub(c1,c2)])])]),
      nop('*'),
      sides([  s(a1,_,_),s(a2,_,_),s(b1,_,_),s(b2,_,_),
               s(c1,_,_),s(c2,_,_)])
      ]))
```

This example illustrates some of the general restrictions on gestalt properties: the DAV max is always attached to the first OS-section (proportion!), whereas the DAV sub is not available for gestalt specification at
all. As gestalt specification takes place independently of an object's position
properties, it does not trigger the assignment of deictic sides.

We can now go on to the CONTEXTUALLY INDUCED SPECIFICATION of a
DAV. Again, a suitable entry in the OS is searched for, that is, an entry that
meets the conditions on possible specification and at the same time satisfies
the restrictions on contextual specification (cf. sections 2.3.2 and 2.4.1
above).

Consider *high pole*. Regarding possible specification, the DAV vert
corresponding to *high* may be attached to the object's OS-section containing
max. Furthermore, specification of max by vert is restricted to objects
whose OS is left unspecified as to verticality. This rules out "tower" (52) or
"wall" (36)(a), but admits "pole" (51) and "brick" (55) for contextually
induced verticality. Contextual specification is accompanied by the assignment of deictic sides that are determined by the DAV in question. Our "high
pole" thus is furnished with deictic top and bottom sides. The following OS
(51') for "high pole" results:

(51') "high pole":

```
os([ dimensions([a,b,c]),
     sections([    section([   axes([a]),
                               boundedness(bounded),
                               endpoints([a1,a2]),
                               assignment([max(a1,a2),vert(a1,a2)])]),
                                           /* length/height */
                   section([   axes([b,c]),
                               boundedness(bounded),
                               endpoints([d1,d2]),
                               assignment([sub(d1,d2)])])]),
                                           /* thickness */
     nop('*'),
     sides([  s(a1,_,d_us), s(a2,_,d_os),s(d1,_,_),s(d2,_,_)]) ])
```

Now we are ready to face the Prolog realization of the three subprocedures of eval_DAP as shown in (57):

(57)

```
identify_DAV(DAP,OS,OSOUT,ASSIGN,ASSIGN,P_NUM):-
    an_assignment(OS,P_NUM,ASSIGN),
    last(ASSIGN,DAV),
    possible_identification(DAV,DAP),
    assign_sides(DAV,OS,OSOUT), !.

gestaltspecify_DAV(DAP,OS,OS,ASSIGN,NewASSIGN,P_NUM):-
    an_assignment(OS,P_NUM,ASSIGN),
    last(ASSIGN,DAV),
    possible_gestaltspecification(DAV,DAP,New_DAV),
    restrictions_on_gestaltspecification(DAP,DAV,OS,P_NUM),
    specify(ASSIGN,New_DAV,NewASSIGN), !.


contextually_specify_DAV(DAP,OS,OSOUT,ASSIGN,NewASSIGN,P_NUM):-
    an_assignment(OS,P_NUM,ASSIGN),
    last(ASSIGN,DAV),
    possible_specification(DAV,DAP,New_DAV),
    restrictions_on_contextual_specification(DAP,DAV,OS,P_NUM),
    specify(ASSIGN,New_DAV,NewASSIGN),
    assign_sides(New_DAV,OS,OSOUT),!.
```

The above Prolog code reveals the modular treatment of constraints governing the COMPATIBILITY CONDITIONS of DAPs and DAVs (cf. section 2.3.2). The matching conditions for identification or specification of a DAV with respect to a DAP (cf. section 2.4.1) and the restrictions on the different specifications are realized by distinct procedures.

Having presented some details of the evaluation of DAPs, we may now take a broader view on the process of interpretation.

First of all, it should be noted that dimensional designation is subject to what is called the 'Principle of one-to-one-Assignment' (cf. Lang 1989: Chap.3). Roughly this means that the interpretation of a DAP (except SIZE, the DAP for *groß* and *klein*) is confined to the identification or specification of a DAV in exactly one of the OS-sections. The interpretation of DAPs and OS has to correspond to a single coherent dimensional and/or positional conceptualization of the object in question. Therefore, it is not possible to interpret two DAPs with respect to the same OS-section (**long high pole*) and thus multiple evaluations have to be ruled out. (58) shows how this is done in OSKAR.

(58)
```
        interpretation(DAP,OSIN,OSOUT,[P_NUM],P_LIST):-
            atom(DAP),
            not(DAP = 'SIZE'),
            eval_DAP(DAP,OSIN,OSOUT,P_NUM,EVAL),
            not(member(P_NUM,P_LIST)).
```

The OS-section number P_NUM, which is instantiated after the successful application of an evaluation rule (cf. (57)), may not be in the list P_LIST of those OS-sections which have already been evaluated. The recursive part of this interpretation procedure, in which P_NUM is inserted into P_LIST, is the following:

(59)
```
        interpretation([],Y,Y,_,Z).
        interpretation([DAP|R],OSIN,OSOUT,_,P_LIST):-
            interpretation(DAP,OSIN,OS1,P_NUMLIST,P_LIST),
            append(P_NUMLIST,P_LIST,NEW_P_LIST),
            interpretation(R,OS1,OSOUT,_,NEW_P_LIST).
```

Nothing has been said by now about the way OSKAR treats contextually induced **reference to the surrounding space** (namely **orientation** and **perspectivization** of an object) in a principled and modular fashion. These are **positional properties** which we might easily cope with by interpreting the DAPs 'VERT' and 'OBS' with respect to an OS in the course of evaluation by means of R3 (contextual specification). Yet we would miss a generalization by focussing on the mere applicability of this rule instead of trying to find out what it tells us when it is used.

For instance, we want to be able to express and represent the fact that certain classes of objects (such as "brick"), which are characteristically unspecified with respect to their surrounding space, can be oriented in different ways[18] Consequently, their various orientations are verbalized in distinct ways: cf. *to set the brick upright* and *to lay the brick down on something*. We therefore prefer a separate module that deals with the various possible orientations and perspectivizations of objects.

For this reason, in OSKAR the procedure that fixes an object's reference to the surrounding space is kept distinct from the interpretation procedure described above. With this distinction on the implementation level (cf.(60)), we are able to model differences existing on the conceptual level such as between "setting upright" and "being upright".

(60)
```
interpretation(DAPs,OS,OSOUT,Message) :-
    reference_to_surrounding_space(OS,OS1,Message),
    interpretation(DAPs,OS1,OSOUT,_,[]).
```

(60) shows the structure of the general interpretation procedure, which can be read as: DAPs are interpreted relative to an object's OS after possibly having fixed a reference to the surrounding space, thereby changing OS into a modified OS'. The variable `Message` will be bound within the predicate `reference_to_surrounding_space` to indicate the spatial position with respect to which the object is interpreted.

Given this, the following cases for establishing or not establishing reference to the surrounding space can be distinguished :

*   reference is not explicitly established:
    the object either has no reference to the surrounding space or must be interpreted with respect to its canonical (**normal**) position (in this case OS and OS' are identical)
*   the object is perspectivized
*   the object is oriented
*   the object is both oriented and perspectivized
*   the object is de-perspectivized (this is the case when e.g. a desk is said to be *long and wide* instead of *wide and deep*)

---

18   These, of course, depend on which axis of the object is aligned to the Vertical.

This full range of variation is accounted for by the procedure `reference_to_surrounding_space` listed in (61):

(61)
```
reference_to_surrounding_space(OS,OS,Message):-
     not(((an_assignment(OS,_,Assign1), /* no vert- or obs- entries */
          member(vert(_,_),Assign1));
         (an_assignment(OS,_,Assign2),
          last(Assign2,obs(_,_))))),
     Message = ['Object lacks reference to the surrounding space'].

reference_to_surrounding_space(OS,OSOUT,Message):-
     an_assignment(OS,_,Assign1),
     member(vert(_,_),Assign1),
     an_assignment(OS,_,Assign2),
     last(Assign2,obs(_,_)),
     perspectivization2(OS,OSOUT),    /* assigning across (see below)*/
     Message = ['Object is in normal position:',
                'canonical reference to the surrounding space',
                'as regards orientation and perspectivization'].

reference_to_surrounding_space(OS,OS,Message):-
     an_assignment(OS,_,Assign1),
     last(Assign1,vert(_,_)),
     not((an_assignment(OS,_,Assign2),last(Assign2,obs(_,_)))),
     Message = ['Object is in normal position:',
                'canonical reference to the surrounding space',
                'as regards orientation'].

reference_to_surrounding_space(OS,OSOUT,Message):-
     an_assignment(OS,_,Assign),
     last(Assign,vert(_,_)),
     perspectivization(OS,OSOUT),
     Message = ['Object is in normal position:',
                'contextually specified with respect',
                'to the Observer-axis'].

reference_to_surrounding_space(OS,OSOUT,Message):-
     not((an_assignment(OS,_,Assign),
         last(Assign,vert(_,_)))),
     perspectivization(OS,OSOUT),
     Message = ['Object is perspectivised:',
                'contextually specified with respect',
                'to the Observer-axis'].

reference_to_surrounding_space(OS,OSOUT,Message):-
     movable(OS),
     orientation(OS,OSOUT),
     Message = ['Object is positioned:',
                'contextually specified with respect',
                'to the Vertical'].

reference_to_surrounding_space(OS,OSOUT,Message):-
     movable(OS),
     orientation(OS,OS1),
     perspectivization(OS1,OSOUT),
     Message = ['Object is positioned:',
                'contextually specified with respect',
                'to the Vertical and to the Observer-axis'].
```

```
reference_to_surrounding_space(OS,OSOUT,Message):-
    movable(OS),
    de_perspectivize(OS,OSOUT),
    Message = ['Object is de-specified with respect to
                 canonical perspectivization'].
```

Obviously, perspectivization and orientation must be taken as operations which change the OS of an object into an OS' that contains the relevant contextual information (in terms of the DAVs vert, obs or across). But this is just the contextually induced specification of the OS described above! Therefore, perspectivization and orientation can be realized by using the third eval_DAP-procedure of (57).

As for **contextual perspectivization**, three cases can be distinguished:

- both obs and across can be contextually assigned (e.g. a board used as a window-sill can be said to be *deep and wide*)[19]
- only obs can be assigned (*deep barrel*)
- only across can be assigned (*wide/*deep book*).

In OSKAR, it looks like this:

(62)
```
perspectivization(OS,OSOUT):-
    perspectivization1(OS,OS1),
    perspectivization2(OS1,OSOUT),!.

perspectivization(OS,OSOUT):-
    perspectivization1(OS,OSOUT).

perspectivization(OS,OSOUT):-
    perspectivization2(OS,OSOUT).

/* obs - assignment !*/
perspectivization1(OS,OSOUT):-
    eval_DAP('OBS',OS,OSOUT,N,spec).

/*across - assignment !*/
perspectivization2(OS,OSOUT):-
    eval_DAP('ACROSS',OS,OSOUT,N,spec).
```

Now to **contextual orientation**. It covers the following cases:

- vert is attached to the first OS-section; this can be interpreted as "setting the object upright"

---

[19]   The simultaneous assignment of obs and across (when it is possible to assign them!) demonstrates the inherent relativity of *across* on the conceptual level: fixing an obs-axis of an object entails fixing the across-axis of the object.

- vert is attached to the last OS-section; this can be interpreted as "laying (down)" the object
- vert is attached to the second of three OS-sections[20].

Even if attachment of vert is not possible (meaning that the objects in question will not get a 'height') we still face the following cases:

- deictic top and bottom sides are assigned to the last OS-section; again this is an instance of "laying (down)" an object (pole, disk, pillow)
- deictic top and bottom sides are assigned to the first OS-section; this would amount to "setting the object on edge" (disk, coin)

Note that, strictly speaking, spherical objects (three-dimensional objects characterized by only one OS-section) cannot be said *to lie* or *stand* (and hence *to be laid down*).[21] So they have to be excluded from the 'layable' objects. Similarly, *setting on edge* can only be used with objects which have a diam or dist entry in the first OS-section and a d_sub entry in the second. However, we will not go into the details of these operations any further, but only list the relevant procedures of OSKAR:

(63)
```
orientation(OS,OSOUT):-
     set_upright(OS,OSOUT).

orientation(OS,OSOUT):-
     eval_DAP('VERT',OS,OSOUT,2,spec).

orientation(OS,OSOUT):-
     lay(OS,OSOUT).

orientation(OS,OSOUT):-
     set_on_edge(OS,OSOUT).


set_upright(OS,OSOUT):-
     eval_DAP('VERT',OS,OSOUT,1,spec).


lay(OS,OSOUT):-
     eval_DAP('VERT',OS,OSOUT,3,spec).
```

---

[20] This case exemplifies a specific area of uncertainty in speakers' intuition: people cannot state unequivocally whether the object *stands* or *lies* in this position.

[21] Another case of uncertain intuitions.

```
lay(OS,OSOUT):-
    not((an_assignment(OS,P_N,ASS),last(ASS,vert(_,_)))),
                         /* no orientation yet */
    not(eval_DAP('VERT',OS,_,3,spec)),
                    /* 'Vert' cannot specify the third OS-section */
    not(is_lying(OS)),      /* the object is not already lying */
    an_assignment(OS,2,_),  /* to exclude balls etc. */
    assignment_in_last_section(OS,ASS1),
    last(ASS1,DAV), DAV =..[_,A1,A2],
                        /* get the endpoints of the last OS-section*/
    assign_deictic_sides(OS,OSOUT,vert,A1,A2).

set_on_edge(OS,OSOUT):-
    not(eval_DAP('VERT',OS,_,_,spec)),
                        /* 'Vert' cannot specify OS */
    an_assignment(OS,1,Assign),
                    /* get the assignment of the first OS-section */
    member(DAV,Assign), DAV =..[DIM,A1,A2], member(DIM,[diam,dist]),
                    /* the assignment must contain a diam or dist */
    an_assignment(OS,2,Assign2),
                        /* to exclude balls etc. */
    assign_deictic_sides(OS,OSOUT,vert,A1,A2).
```

Since we have clarified the notion "contextual specification" by explicating the operations of fixing a reference to the surrounding space for any as yet unspecified objects, we no longer need the specification rule of evaluating a DAP as an interpretation rule. Therefore, interpreting a DAP with respect to an OS always means evaluating it by identification. This is expressed in (58'), the slightly modified version of (58).

(58')

```
interpretation(DAP,OSIN,OSOUT,[P_NUM],P_LIST):-
    atom(DAP),
    not(DAP = 'SIZE'),
    eval_DAP(DAP,OSIN,OSOUT,P_NUM,ident),
    not(member(P_NUM,P_LIST)).
```

Now we can summarize how the DAPs and OS interact: the DAPs are interpreted with respect to OS by identifying the pertinent DAVs in an OS'; OS and OS' are identical if no reference to the surrounding space exists or needs to be fixed (i.e. the object is canonically oriented or perspectivized); otherwise, OS is transformed into OS' by specifying the relevant DAVs thereby establishing or fixing the object's reference to the surrounding space (i.e. **positioning** the object). The structure of this interaction of DAPs and OS is depicted in Fig. 11.

Fig.11   Interpretation of DAPs and OS

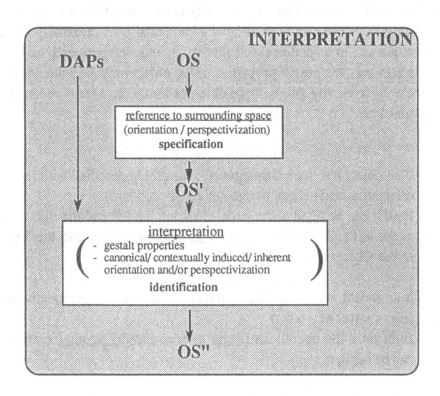

3.3.2   Changing the Position of Objects

In the previous section we have described how dimensional designation is treated in OSKAR when the object is either unspecified with respect to the surrounding space or is in its **normal** position. So far nothing has been said about what a **non-normal** position of an object could be. Obviously "being in a non-normal position" is not defined for objects with inherent reference to the surrounding space ("hole") or with no such reference ("brick"). In light of that, a non-normal position of an object must result from **changing its (normal) position**. In this section, we will explain how these changes can be modelled by appropriate modifications of the object's OS.

In OSKAR, positioning an object and changes of an object's position have a parallel realization. This, we claim, makes an important contribution to some aspects of the conceptual analysis of lexical items that express such changes as, say, verbs like *tilt to the back / the front / the left / over, turn to the back / the front / the left / around* etc.

There are a number of prerequisites and rules that determine the range of positional changes an object may be subject to. First of all, the object must be **movable**. Moreover, it must have a canonical or contextually induced orientation and/or a canonical or contextually induced perspectivization. In addition to this, the gestalt properties of the object must be suitable. Based on these features, the range of possible positional changes is reduced to a few rules like:

- **if** an object has three disintegrated axes **and** is specified with regard to orientation and perspectivization (e.g. a cupboard)
  then it can be <u>tilted</u> to the back, the front, the left and the right; <u>turned</u> to the left and the right or <u>turned around</u> (with regard to the Vertical or the Observer-axis)[22]

- **if** an object is specified for orientation **but** not for perspectivization (e.g. a tower or a table)
  then only the operations <u>tilting over</u> or <u>turning around</u> (vertically) can be applied

- **if** an object's first OS-section contains `diam` or `dist` **and** the second is specified for orientation (e.g. an ash-tray or a coin)
  then it can be <u>set on edge</u>

- **if** an object has three disintegrated axes, the second or third of which is specified with regard to orientation (e.g. a desk),
  then it can be <u>set on its side</u>

(64) shows the general structure of the relevant module of OSKAR.

(64)
```
change_of_position(OS,OSOUT,'Object is tilted !'):-
    tilt(OS,OSOUT).

change_of_position(OS,OSOUT,'Object is tilted over !'):-
    tilt_over(OS,OSOUT).
```

---

22   Due to the relevance of orthogonality for the system of spatial axes, "tilting" and "turning" in OSKAR proceed in (possibly iterated) steps of 90°. Clearly these are only special instances of the concepts of "tilting" and "turning".

```
change_of_position(OS,OSOUT,'Object is turned !'):-
    turn(OS,OSOUT).

change_of_position(OS,OSOUT,'Object is turned around !'):-
    turn_around(OS,OSOUT).

change_of_position(OS,OSOUT,'Object is set on edge !'):-
    set_on_edge(OS,OSOUT).

change_of_position(OS,OSOUT,'Object is set on its side!'):-
    set_on_side(OS,OSOUT).
```

Similar to the corresponding positioning procedures shown in (63), set_on_edge and set_on_side are simply realized by specifying an orientation in the first OS-section of the given OS, but with the slight difference that any current vert entry has to be removed first. We therefore need not elaborate on them any further. Instead, we shall explain the operations of 'tilting' and 'turning' in some detail.

As mentioned in section 3.2, the introduction of axis endpoints as part of the OS-representations has made it possible to account for axis directions. This now becomes relevant for the realization of the various positional changes ('tilting' and 'turning' by 90°), which can be described by the following general pattern:

- remove two of the DAVs vert, obs or across from the OS
- change the direction in one of these OS-sections
- re-specify the removed DAVs, but with their places exchanged

This pattern illustrates the fact that in each case, two of the three OS-sections are involved in the stepwise change of an object's position. Re-specification is carried out by an application of eval_DAP so that the correct reassignment of deictic sides is carried out automatically. An example for 'tilting to the right' is depicted in Fig. 12.

Fig.12   Change of Assignments with "Tilting an Object to the Right"

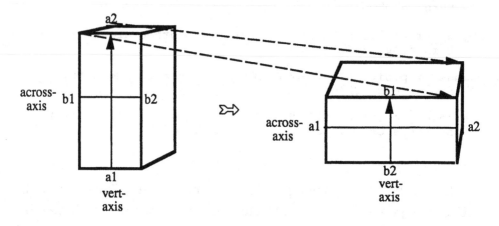

We can thus posit the following rules for "tilting" and "turning", relying exclusively on combinations of DAVs and axial endpoints (the arrow indicates the transition to the ensuing state):

(65a) **tilting to the front:**
       <vert(A1,A2),obs(B1,B2)>   ⇨   <obs(A2,A1),vert(B1,B2)>

(65b) **tilting to the back:**
       <vert(A1,A2),obs(B1,B2)>   ⇨   <obs(A1,A2),vert(B2,B1)>

(65c) **tilting to the right:**
       <vert(A1,A2),across(B1,B2)> ⇨   <across(A1,A2),vert(B2,B1)>

(65d) **tilting to the left:**
       <vert(A1,A2),across(B1,B2)> ⇨   <across(A2,A1),vert(B1,B2)>

(65e) **turning to the right:**
       <obs(A1,A2),across(B1,B2)> ⇨   <across(A2,A1),obs(B1,B2)>

(65f) **turning to the left:**
       <obs(A1,A2),across(B1,B2)> ⇨   <across(A1,A2),obs(B2,B1)>

To give an example of the realization of these rules in OSKAR, (66) shows the procedure `tilt_to_the_right`.

(66)

```
tilt_to_the_right(OS,OSOUT):-
    remove_contextual_specification(vert,P_NUM1,OS,OS1,same),
    remove_contextual_specification(across,P_NUM2,OS1,OS2,reverse),
    eval_DAP('VERT',OS2,OS3,P_NUM2,spec),
    eval_DAP('ACROSS',OS3,OSOUT,P_NUM1,spec),!.
```

As in the case of the positioning procedures discussed in the previous section, eval_DAP is used to fix an object's reference to the surrounding space. The removal of the relevant contextual entries is always performed by remove_contextual_specification, which in addition may change the endpoints of the OS-sections (reverse) or leave them untouched (same). The various ways in which an object may rotate can now easily be modelled by applying specific subsets of the rules in (65)[23] The relevant explicitly lexicalized cases of object rotation include:

(66a)   **turning around**:
         applying (65e) or (65f) twice

(66b)   **turning over**:
         applying any of (65a) - (65f) at least once

(66c)   **turning upside down**:
    1)   applying any of (65a) - (65f) twice
    2)   In case an obs entry is not available in any OS-section, "turning over" or "turning upside down" are realized by the following rule, which only exchanges the vertical endpoints:
         <vert(A1,A2)>   ⟹   <vert(A2,A1)>

(66d)   **tilting over**:
    1)   remove the vert entry from an OS-section and re-specify 'VERT' with respect to another, less prominent OS-section
    2)   if such an OS-section is not available as a landing site for the removed vert, then "tilting over" is effected merely by re-assigning deictic top and bottom sides

(65) and (66) exhaust all possible cases of rotation.

---

[23]   The presentation given below is adapted to English verbs of rotation. Their German counterparts *umdrehen* and *umkippen* pick out slightly different subsets from (65) but are handled without any problem in OSKAR.

Having explained the realization in OSKAR of the various positional changes of objects, we may now consider their role in the interaction of DAPs and OS. Since the interpretation of the DAPs with respect to an object's non-normal position is just another case of the general interpretation procedure, all we need to do is add a second clause, leaving us with the final version shown in (67).

(67)
```
interpretation(DAPs,OS,OSOUT,Message):-
    reference_to_surrounding_space(OS,OS1,Message),
    interpretation(DAPs,OS1,OSOUT,_,[]).

interpretation(DAPs,OS,OSOUT,Message):-
    orientation_in_section(OS,_),
    change_of_position(OS,OS1,Message),
    interpretation(DAPs,OS1,OSOUT,_,[]).
```

The structure of the interaction of DAPs and OS presented so far is summarized in Fig. 13.

Fig. 13   Interpretation of DAPs and OS (elaborate)

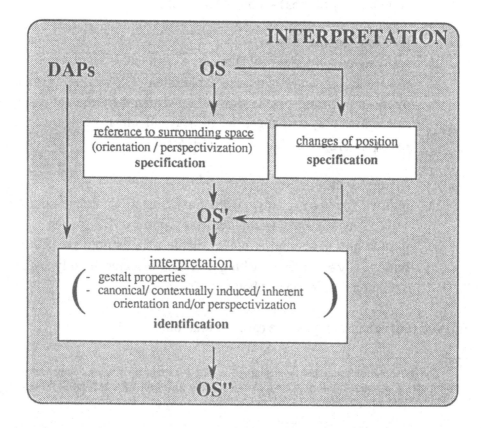

3.3.3   Position Properties

There is another aspect of spatial knowledge which is now representable in OSKAR: the characteristics of an object's position, which constitute an essential part of the meaning of such expressions as *standing, lying, upside down* etc. It is evident that these (static) **position properties** are closely related to the (dynamic) positioning or positional change of objects discussed in the previous sections, in that they refer to the results of those operations (i.e. to the **position** of the objects). In this section, we will describe their representation in OSKAR.

Again, an object's movability is the prerequisite for having positional properties at all[24] This is confirmed by the unacceptable sentences in (68)(a) and (b):

(68)   (a) *The hill stands in the countryside*
         (b) *The hill lies in the countryside*

These examples show that immobile objects cannot have a <u>position</u> but only a <u>location</u>. Thus, confined to movable objects, the following rules can be formulated:

An object

- **is lying** if
  its most prominent axis is <u>not</u> aligned to the Vertical (i.e. if it lacks a vert entry in its first OS-section) **and**
  - intrinsic and deictic orientations are each assigned to different axes of the object (e.g. a cupboard tilted over) **or**
  - there is only a deictic orientation for the second or third OS-section (this excludes *lying balls* but allows for *lying poles*)

- **is standing** if
  - an OS-section contains a vert entry and the intrinsic and deictic orientations coincide at that OS-section (a desk in normal position) **or**

---

24   Much use has been made hitherto of this concept and its representational counterpart, the predicate 'movable'. We will come back to this in section 3.5.

- there is only a deictic orientation which is not assigned to the least prominent axis (a coin standing on edge)

- **is upside down** if the intrinsic and deictic vertical sides are assigned to the same OS-section but do not coincide

- **is reversed** if the non-vertical intrinsic and deictic sides are pairwise assigned to the same OS-section but do not coincide (a picture turned to the wall)

These rules account for the aforementioned intuitive uncertainties. Spherical objects are excluded because they do not have `vert` entry and have only one OS-section; hence they neither can stand nor lie. Objects with three disintegrated axes and no intrinsic assignments which happen to have a contextually induced `vert` in their second OS-section simultaneously fulfill both the rules for standing and lying (as may be the case for a brick). Another kind of uncertainty may be observed for objects like ash trays when they are 'upside down'. Are they lying or standing? Speakers typically avoid a decision by using the simple copula: *The ash tray is upside down on the table.*

Position properties are realized in OSKAR as one-place predicates whose arguments are object schemata. As an example, the procedure implementing the 'is lying'-rule is presented in (69).

(69)
```
is_lying(OS):-
    orientation_in_section(OS,P_NUM),
    not(P_NUM = 1),
    intrinsic_Vertical_in_section(OS,P_NUM1),
    not(P_NUM = P_NUM1).

is_lying(OS):-
    not(intrinsic_Vertical_in_section(OS,_)),
    orientation_in_section(OS,P_NUM),
    not(P_NUM = 1).
```

Of course, the last word on the rules for positional properties has yet to be spoken. What has to be worked out in detail is the Semantic Form of the verbs of position along the lines of the analysis of the adjectives as presented in section 2.2.2. At any rate, we have demonstrated that such an analysis is anticipated in the procedures by means of which OSKAR treats the position properties of objects.

3.4 The Overall Structure of OSKAR

Having presented the relevant components of OSKAR individually, we may now link them together in the overall structure of the program. By doing so, we will reveal the processing aspects of OSKAR, which have not been considered so far.

We make use of the position properties described in the previous section by allowing for a position property (POSITION) to be specified in the Input. After successful interpretation of the DAPs and the OS, the property POSITION is tested for validity with respect to the object schema OS"[25] If this is not the case, then a(nother) change of position is simulated until no more possibilities remain. The same is done if the initial interpretation of DAPs with respect to OS is not successful.

There are various reasons why an interpretation may fail. For instance, because the DAPs and OS in question are incompatible on general grounds (cf. *long ball*), or because a DAP is inapplicable to an object in a given position (cf. *long tower* when the tower is in normal position). OSKAR is designed to produce a diagnostic error message for any failure.

---

[25] We speak of 'testing' a certain position property because we want to keep this distinct from the theoretical notion of the 'interpretation' of dimensional properties. For the same reason, we use a menu as a means for selecting a position property to be tested. The default value for POSITION is `no_position_specified`, with which the test procedure always succeeds.

Fig. 14   The Overall Structure of OSKAR

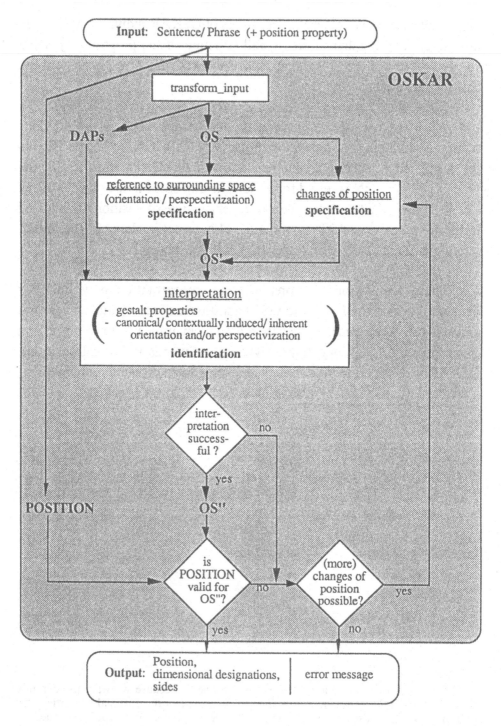

Here are a few examples given as Input-Output pairs:

Input: *long pole*   (no position specified)

Output: Object lacks reference to the surrounding space
/* first solution */

```
Section 1:     [max(a1, a2)]
Section 2:     [sub(d1, d2)]

sides:         s(a1, _1326, _1327)
               s(a2, _1333, _1334)
               s(d1, _1340, _1341)
               s(d2, _1347, _1348)
```

Object is positioned:
contextually specified with respect to the Vertical
/* second solution: the pole is set upright */

```
Section 1:     [max(a1, a2), |, vert(a1, a2)]26
Section 2:     [sub(d1, d2)]

sides:         s(a1, _1326, d_us)
               s(a2, _1333, d_os)
               s(d1, _1340, _1341)
               s(d2, _1347, _1348)
```

Object is positioned:
contextually specified with respect to the Vertical
/* third solution: the pole is laid (down) */

```
Section 1:     [max(a1, a2)]
Section 2:     [sub(d1, d2)]

sides:         s(a1, _1326, _1327)
               s(a2, _1333, _1334)
               s(d1, _1524, d_us)
               s(d2, _1529, d_os)
```

Input: *long pole*   **(standing)**

Output: Object is positioned:
contextually specified with respect to the Vertical

```
Section 1:     [max(a1, a2), |, vert(a1, a2)]
Section 2:     [sub(d1, d2)]

sides:         s(a1, _1326, d_us)
               s(a2, _1333, d_os)
               s(d1, _1340, _1341)
               s(d2, _1347, _1348)
```

---

26   The vertical bar separates the primary from the contextually induced DAVs.

Input: **high** *pole*   (no position specified)

Output: Object is positioned:
           contextually specified with respect to the Vertical

           Section 1:   [max(a1, a2), |, **vert**(a1, a2)]
           Section 2:   [sub(d1, d2)]

           sides: s(a1, _1836, **d_us**)
                          s(a2, _1843, **d_os**)
                          s(d1, _1850, _1851)
                          s(d2, _1857, _1858)

Input: *long tower*   (no position specified)

Output: Object is tilted over !

           Section 1:   [max(a1, a2)]
           Section 2:   [sub(d1, d2)]

           sides :   s(a1, i_us, _2204)
                          s(a2, i_os, _1905)
                          s(d1, _2365, **d_us**)
                          s(d2, _2370, **d_os**)

Input: *deep pole*   (no position specified)

Output: The object cannot be interpreted with respect to the given
           dimensional designation(s)!

Input: high pole   (lying)

Output: The object cannot be interpreted with respect to the given
           dimensional designation(s) and the position property!

And so on through OSKAR's generous grab-bag of the world's objects...

3.5   Some Further Aspects of OSKAR

3.5.1   Object Categorization

It can be directly inferred from the previous presentation of OSKAR that the program classifies objects as to their dimensionable gestalt and position properties. For example, given the Input *long object* or *high and thick object*, OSKAR will enumerate, based on the appropriate object schemata, all instances of "long object" or "high and thick object" available in its inventory of object knowledge. In addition to that, the information contained in the object schemata allow for further-reaching classifications among spatial objects.

As a welcome supplement to existing proposals for **ontological hierarchies**, OSKAR provides us with a set of basics on which an ontological taxonomy of objects can be built in quite a natural way. At issue are some of the criteria underlying the so-called **sortal concepts** in object ontologies.

As should be clear by now, the structure of an OS as a representational format of object concepts as well as the inventory of OS-types implicitly incorporate ontological distinctions. These distinctions, in particular those based on boundedness, dimensionality and mobility of objects, provide a ready means for defining and refining ontological categories, see Fig. 8.

Thus the **boundedness/unboundedness**-dichotomy is immediately obtainable from the boundedness-features of the OS-sections.

Likewise, the classifications of objects as **0D, 1D, 2D, or 3D objects** can be directly inferred from the dimensions-feature.

Immobile objects are those which
- are either one- or two-dimensional because they are conceived as designated parts of three-dimensional objects (e.g. "edge", "face");
- do not contain a DAV empty in their oriented OS-section; as the DAV empty is the unspecified landing site for contextual specification, it has to be present for an object to be tilted, i.e. moved. Thus, e.g. "hill" is excluded from being "tilted".

- • are inherently perspectivized (i.e. contain an iobs-entry in one of their OS-sections); this reflects the fact that an object with inherent depth (e.g. "hole", "wound") cannot be moved independently of its carrier.

All other kinds of objects are movable.

3.5.2 Handling *groß* and *klein*

The details of this topic would go far beyond the scope of this paper (see Lang 1987, 1989: Chap. 5 for a detailed discussion). Nevertheless we want to present the most important distinction which has to be made concerning the use of German *groß* and *klein* (with their DAP 'SIZE'). There are two kinds of interpretations of those adjectives:

(70) (a) the GLOBAL INTERPRETATION, where all dimensions of the given object are involved, to the exclusion of other dimensional designations - as in (71);

    (b) the PARTIALLY RESTRICTED INTERPRETATION, where other cooccurring dimensional adjectives restrict the range of dimensions covered by 'SIZE' - as in (72).

(71)   *ein großes Haus* (a big house)
(72)   *ein großes, aber ziemlich niedriges Haus*
    (a large but rather low house)[27]
(73)   **large snow*

As (73) shows, both interpretations are restricted to bounded objects. The difference between the interpretations can be sketched as follows:

The global interpretation does not refer to any kind of additive or multiplicative combinations of single axis extents but to the holistically accessed global impression of the object. This, in turn, is related to what might be called the NORMAL PROPORTION. The NORMAL PROPORTION can be modelled in OSKAR by setting a value to the attribute 'nop' in the object's OS.

---

27   Note that the various interpretations of German *groß* are lexicalized differently in English (e.g. *tall, large, big*).

The same does not hold for partial interpretations. Instead, we have to identify the single dimensions of the object being addressed by 'SIZE' in order to exclude them from further interpretation. For three-dimensional objects this amounts to identifying the two most prominent axes, whether disintegrated (*large flat house*) or integrated (*large flat disk*). In OSKAR, the scope of interpretations of 'SIZE' is accounted for by the following additional interpretation rules:

(74)
```
interpretation('SIZE',OS,OS,[1,2,3],[]):-
    number_of_sections(OS,3),
    not((a_section(OS,P,SEC),
        get_boundedness_of_section(SEC,unbounded))),
    get_nop(OS,_).

interpretation('SIZE',OS,OS,[1,2],P_LIST):-
    number_of_sections(OS,2),
    not((a_section(OS,P,SEC),
        get_boundedness_of_section(SEC,unbounded))),
    get_nop(OS,_).

interpretation('SIZE',OS,OS,[1],P_LIST):-
    number_of_sections(OS,1),
    not(one_dimensional(OS)),
    not((a_section(OS,P,SEC),
        get_boundedness_of_section(SEC,unbounded))),
    get_nop(OS,_).

interpretation('SIZE',OS,OSOUT,[1,2],P_LIST):-
                                    /* partial interpretation */
    a_section(OS,3,_),
    eval_DAP('*',OS,OS1,1,ident),
    not(member(1,P_LIST)),
    eval_DAP('*',OS1,OSOUT,2,ident),
    not(member(2,P_LIST)),!.

interpretation('SIZE',OS,OSOUT,[1],P_LIST):-
                                    /* partial interpretation */
    integratedness_of_section(OS,1,int),
    a_section(OS,2,_),
    eval_DAP('*',OS,OSOUT,1,ident),
    not(member(1,P_LIST)),!.
```

3.5.3   Commensurability of Objects

Having come to grips with the partially restricted interpretation of 'SIZE', we now have the means to treat comparisons of object sizes as illustrated by the comparative expressions in (75/76).

(75)   *This car is bigger than that car*
(76)   (*)*The car is bigger than the pole*

Obviously sentence (76) is unacceptable, the reason being that the objects are not **commensurable** (i.e. comparable with respect to their dimensional extents). In other words, there is no 'common share' for comparison. Note that this 'common share' need not include all dimensional designations of the objects under comparison as in (75) but a relevant section of them.

(77) and (78) demonstrate that the object may even have a different dimensionality. In these cases, *parking lot* and *garage door* determine length and width and width and height, respectively, as the 'common share'; that is, the OS-sections with respect to which *car* is to be partially interpreted.

(77)   *The car is too big for the parking lot*
(78)   *The car is too big for the garage door*

We have provided for commensurability of objects in OSKAR by allowing Inputs which satisfy the pattern 'OBJECT 1 is COMPARATIVE-ADJECTIVE than OBJECT 2'. There are procedures which test the commensurability of the objects to be compared and determine whether they are comparable on all or only on selected dimensions. In the latter case the relevant OS-sections are marked as being involved in the comparison.

3.5.4   Entailments

In order to account for the entailments discussed in section 2.4.2 above (e.g. that *the pole is 3m high* entails *the pole is 3m long*), another Input pattern (79) was added to OSKAR, allowing for natural language Input like (80).

(79)   Is NOUN PHRASE1 derivable from NOUN PHRASE2 ?
(80)   *Is a long pole derivable from a high pole?*

(81)   *high pole* $\longrightarrow$ *long pole*
(82)   *high tower* $\nrightarrow$ *long tower*
(83)   *high hill* $\nrightarrow$ **long hill*

The Input pattern (79) is processed in two steps. First, both NOUN PHRASES are interpreted as described in section 3.3. Then the pertinent

OS-sections of the object schemata are compared. For the inference to be valid they have to match. This is the case if they are identical per se, or if they become identical by properly **de-specifying** one of them - cf. (81) vs. (82) and (83).

De-specification simply means removing the contextual specification from the OS-section in question. This procedure accounts for the clear validity of (81), marks the conditional acceptability of (82) in an indirect way, but rules out (83) altogether. The reasons are obvious: a tower has a canonical orientation which, by definition, cannot be de-specified. The marked interpretation of *long tower* (suggesting that the tower is tilted over) has been discussed above. A hill, however, has a fixed vertical orientation that makes it inaccessible to maximality assignment.

3.6   Extensions and Prospects

Having presented the program OSKAR and its theoretical foundation, we now want to give a short outlook on what <u>can</u> and, hopefully, <u>will</u> be done to expand on our accomplishments thus far. OSKAR, the outcome of linking linguistics with computation, can be extended in various respects within both fields.

Practical applications

In view of the details exhaustively handled by OSKAR, it seems highly plausible that the program could make a useful contribution if embedded into a <u>tutorial system</u> for language learning. The lexical field of dimensional adjectives and related expressions is part of the core lexicon and hence of the basic vocabulary to be mastered by any foreign language student. As it accounts for all the subtleties of dimensional designation and positional variation, OSKAR might well serve as a resource for tutorial programs in computer aided education.[28]

In this context, another idea comes to mind. Provided that OSKAR is furnished with a graphic component that would allow for OS information to be presented as pictures of objects on the screen, further interesting applications would emerge. For instance, the program thus enhanced could be used for a variety of <u>experimental purposes</u> in psycholinguistics such as object naming tasks or object recognition tests.

---

[28] We owe this suggestion to Chr. Habel (personal communication).

Theoretical Aspects

From Dimensions to Distances. As OSKAR is focussed on object properties, it is devoted to that subset of spatial knowledge which concerns **small-scale space**. In this sense, object schemata have to be regarded as object-centered representations. The object properties thus rendered are ultimately reducible to geometric notions. In order to account for the entire scope of spatial knowledge, the theory and the program have to be properly extended. That is, the OS must be combined with representations for the configurations of, and relations between, objects in **large-scale space** (as expressed by e.g. local prepositions and adverbs). To account for that, we need a suitable interface to representations based on topology. Note that the side assignments in the OS may help us bridge the gap between the different domains of spatial cognition. In a way, they form the hinge between topology and geometry, which together determine the structure of spatial knowledge.

From Adjectives to Verbs and Prepositions. The procedures for positioning, positional properties, and positional change of objects ("lay down", "lying", "turn over", etc.) outlined in section 3.3 contain, in essence, the conditions determining the meaning of individual verbs of position. These conditions provide the conceptual basis for constructing an appropriate semantics for this lexical group. For a detailed study of position verbs along these lines, see Maienborn 1990.

The analysis of local prepositions might profit from the information coded in the OS. Take the so-called projective prepositions (*above/below*, *in front of - behind, right/left of* etc.). These involve the localization of an object x with respect to a preposition-specific neighbourhood region of some reference object y. For reference objects having intrinsically assigned object sides (provided by their OS - see section 2.3.4 and Fig. 8), the neighbourhood region is determined by the respective intrinsic top, bottom, front, or rear. Reference objects lacking intrinsically designated sides are assigned front, rear etc., and hence neighbourhood regions, from an external source, which amounts to the so-called deictic (or, more generally, extrinsic) side-assignment. The details about the way these devices determine neighbourhood regions by making use of OS-information of the reference objects involved are discussed in Lang (1990b).

4. The Integration of OSKAR into the LILOG System

4.1 Taking Stock

The highlights of the foregoing chapters are the Prolog program OSKAR and its theoretical foundation — a theory about knowledge of spatial objects that is significant for cognitive linguistics and artificial intelligence. At the same time, we have been using the "rapid prototyping" method in order to facilitate the transition from theory to practice. To summarize the two stages achieved thus far:

(i) development of a <u>linguistic theory</u> based on the analysis of natural language expressions (Chap. 2);
(ii) creation of a <u>prototype</u> that tests, refines and possibly extends that theory (Chap. 3).

This chapter will round out the process by illustrating the third stage: the <u>integration</u> of OSKAR's representations and procedures into the natural language comprehension system of the LILOG project. Though the case study in this chapter draws on the LEU/2 prototype, we will simply refer to the LILOG system in the following.

The prototype OSKAR serves as a guide for bridging the gap between natural language processing (NLP) and knowledge representation (KR); it confirms the "small is beautiful" maxim of AI research advocated by Patel-Schneider (1984). According to this principle, a KR system benefits from excluding as many dimensions as possible in order to explore a single problem area with depth and generality, rather than taking the "micro-worlds" approach in which (often shallow) analyses of many phenomena are attempted for a limited domain. OSKAR provides us with a detailed representational format for spatial properties of objects and demonstrates the way those properties interact with language in a setup that is neutral with respect to other problem areas. For example, the program indicates some of the features that a KR system will need with respect to object classification, the context dependency of semantic processing, and default assumptions about object properties, without bothering with the details of a classifier, representations of contexts, or a default reasoner. These matters must be taken up by a system such as LILOG that encompasses OSKAR's strategies, in accordance with its specific resources and the goals it is intended to fulfill.

The LILOG system is designed to perform syntactic and semantic analysis of texts in German, resulting in knowledge representations that are used to answer questions about the texts in a natural language dialogue. One of the goals of the project is to achieve a maximum of **task independence**. That is, the representational framework should not be restricted to a specific scenario or domain of knowledge. Instead, the system is organized in such a way that its "high-level" structure can be adapted to as many different domains of application as possible. To that end, the taxonomy of entities that the system "knows about" is designed to be flexible and easily extendible. Furthermore, the representation of **spatial and temporal knowledge** extracted from texts is intended to be highly robust, in that it anticipates a wide variety of phenomena in those domains.

In the next section, we will take a closer look at the strategies established in the LILOG system to achieve these goals, and it will be argued that we can contribute to their fulfillment by adopting the theory of meaning outlined in Chapter 2 above. Section 4.3 contains a brief description of LLILOG, the representational formalism used in LILOG. Finally, sections 4.4 - 4.7 sketch the re-implementation of object schemata in LLILOG, and show how the "loose ends" left hanging by OSKAR are tied up in the LILOG environment.

4.2   Modularity of Linguistic Meaning and Knowledge Representation

The approach to meaning composition presented in 2.1.2 above, according to which a grammatical structure G interacts with a conceptual structure C to yield the meaning of linguistic expressions, is an important theoretical standpoint in cognitive science. But what are the benefits of making this structural distinction in a knowledge representation system? In particular, what is to be gained by assuming object schemata (OS) as a representational format in a text comprehension system like LILOG?

It is not unusual to find KR systems where object dimensions are simply labelled by attributes such as "length", "width", "thickness", and so on — very much in the spirit of a semantic marker framework. These are indeed much simpler than object schemata, but the empirical findings presented in 2.1.3 ought to have made it clear that such an approach is insufficient and cannot be generalized: there is no one-to-one mapping of dimensional terms onto object axes. Now if the dimensional properties of objects are unimportant in some application, then perhaps we could retain the simple solution and live with the idiosyncratic errors that the resulting system is likely to make. But such a treatment runs afoul for reasons of principle and is therefore useless for LILOG (or any comparable system). Note that we have to anticipate texts in which information about the measurable extents and position properties of objects may be of crucial importance. Thus from a purely practical standpoint, we have to have a solution that is theoretically well-founded; hence the importance of a prototype for verifying the correctness of the theory.

Besides the correctness of the solution, however, there are further advantages to be gained by adopting object schemata. An attractive feature of the theory from a linguistic standpoint is the fact that for each dimensional term, there is only one representation at the semantic level (see 2.1.5 above); this makes it attractive for the needs of a task-independent KR system as well. Although dimensional terms are very "commonplace" expressions, the empirical evidence has shown that their behaviour is very subtle and complex, like that of any item in the core vocabulary of a language. Such complexity is often accounted for by assuming distinct semantic representations for every nuance of a word's meaning. Reconsidering the example *breites Brett* [*wide board*] from 2.1.5, we might think of defining a family of object-specific predicates WIDE$_{BOARD}$, WIDE$_{TABLE}$, WIDE$_{TUNNEL}$ and so on, each with its own set of rules for picking out an object dimension, depending on the kind of object in question. These would be necessary to describe the inferences that can be drawn when objects are repositioned (such as the fact that a flagpole which is *5m tall* can be said to be *5m long* when it is lying on the ground; cf. (20) above). The problem is that such inferences are valid for certain kinds of objects but not for others.

But postulating object-specific predicates would be a very undesirable strategy for LILOG in view of the project goals stated above. A system that is conceived this way could only accomodate the objects already defined in its knowledge base; any new class of objects would require new predicates and new rules to be written, tested and debugged. This means that each transition to a new domain of objects would be accompanied by a non-trivial knowledge engineering effort. Of course, one might try to define some broader class of objects (say "rectangular solids") and treat them with a uniform set of rules and predicates. But there is more to dimensional designation of objects than elementary geometry, as Chap. 2 has shown; and, in general, without a systematic underlying theory there is no guarantee that such ad-hoc decisions will always succeed.

The problem is resolved in LILOG by combining the modular approach to the meaning of dimensional expressions with a suitably modular organization of the object ontology. In LILOG as in many other AI projects, a hierarchical taxonomy is assumed (the formalism will be described in detail in the next section). It is a well-known fact of life in AI that a KR system requires a great deal of specific knowledge about the specific kinds of entities and relationships appearing in each individual application. Much of the specific knowledge defined for one application will be completely useless for the next, but certain regularities can be expected to turn up in most, perhaps even all domains. In LILOG, this is dealt with by assuming stable and highly general classes of entities, such as OBJECT and EVENT, at a high level in the taxonomy (the **upper structure** of the hierarchy), for which rules can be written that are expected to be valid in any application. Domain-specific classes of entities (such as boards, tunnels, and poles) are defined at a low level of the hierarchy (the **lower structure**), so that they inherit properties of their superordinate concepts but allow for more specific descriptions (cf. Fig. 15). Thus a single upper structure and the rules that apply to it are retained for the analysis of arbitrary texts, whereas various lower structures can be defined for specific tasks and exchanged when necessary (for a more detailed discussion of task independence and the upper and lower structure in LILOG's taxonomy, see Klose/von Luck (1990, 1991)).

Fig. 15   Upper and Lower Structure in the LILOG Ontology

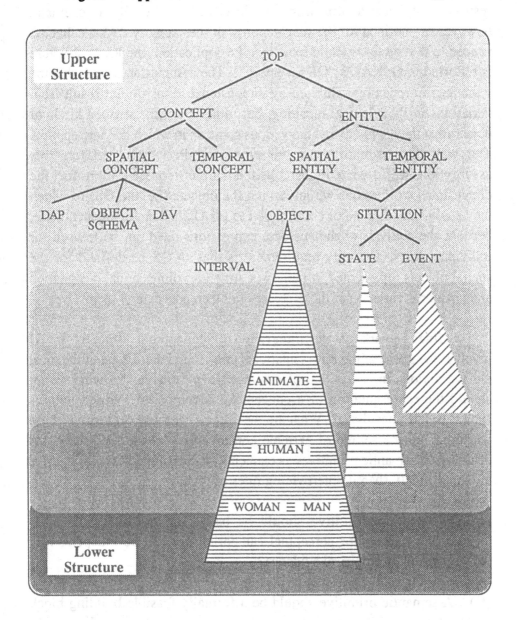

We take advantage of this strategy by stipulating that the scope of application of dimensional terms is restricted to the category OBJECT located in the upper structure of the hierarchy (cf. Fig. 8 in Chap. 2). The stock of dimensional expressions is made available in the system by the inventory of Dimensional Assignment Parameters (DAPs) as shown in section 3.2. above. A generally valid set of rules evaluates DAPs with respect to OS, just as this was done in OSKAR. The object schemata, however, are defined for the subcategories of the category OBJECT that are needed in the lower structure for a specific application (the lower structure is reflected in OSKAR's "OS inventory"). The assumption here is that the variations in meaning exhibited by dimensional terms do not result from variations in their lexical meaning, but rather from the various kinds of objects that they apply to and the various contexts in which they are applied. The way dimensional terms are processed in LILOG reflects this assumption well; we can establish a stable representation for the dimensional expressions while varying the objects (i.e. the OS) to which they apply. This is a major contribution to LILOG's domain independence, because the analysis of dimensional expressions need not be revised for individual texts. The only requirement is that an OS be defined for the spatial objects represented in the lower structure; dimensional designation and positional variation of those objects will then take care of themselves.

A final remark on the integration of conceptual structure in AI involves the status of the representational units found there. One of the most elusive notions in KR is that of a **semantic primitive**. To what extent should the representation of a concept be decomposed? Which notions should be left unanalyzed? What are the criteria for these decisions? These questions are the source of extreme controversy.[29] As to the criteria for deciding on semantic primitives as elements of formal reconstruction, there are three widely shared, intertwining rules of thumb:

(I)   A semantic primitive should be based on intuitively plausible conceptual and/or perceptual categories that can be independently justified by empirical evidence.

(II)   A semantic primitive should be a formally feasible building block whose appropriateness in capturing a given range of phenomena depends on its place in the system.

---

[29]   An excellent discussion of these issues can be found in Hayes (1985), who places emphasis on the third criterion. Indeed, **IPS** and **PPS** from 2.2.1 above can be viewed as an answer to Hayes' plea for a "naive physics" of the gestalt and position properties of objects.

(III)   A semantic primitive should play a part in the description of a broad range of phenomena; various related phenomena should be describable by varying subsets of a common set of primitives.

The present theory provides a framework for getting at some answers. Notice first that the conceptual and the semantic level of interpretation each has its own inventory of primitives. With the conceptual system C, we have a level of knowledge that is language-independent, intermodally accessible, and whose content is based on perception and other cognitive systems; by their very nature, the representational primitives of C should satisfy (I). The primitive units under consideration, namely the Dimension Assignment Values (DAVs), correspond to conceptual categories obtained from **IPS** and **PPS** discussed in 2.2.1 above (maximality, axial symmetry, verticality, etc.). They form the building blocks of object schemata in the sense of rule (II). They are primitive on that level, but not necessarily atomic; for example, they might be analyzed further with respect to their geometric properties in a depictional component of spatial knowledge. On the linguistic level of semantic representation, however, the pertinent set of building blocks is established by the Dimension Assignment Parameters (DAPs), whose status as primitives in the sense of (II) and (III) is determined by the organization of the lexical field of dimension terms.

The important point is that these two sets of level-specific primitives and their interaction are necessary and sufficient to describe dimensional and positional properties of objects as expressed in <u>language</u>. As mentioned above, OSKAR is a guide for the transition from natural language to knowledge representation; any decomposition beyond the level of object schemata is a matter of KR on its own.

We have already seen that object schemata are useful not only for the analysis of dimensional expressions, but also for tackling verbs denoting change of position and/or location (*tilt*, *move*, *roll*, etc.), as well as spatial prepositions. The interesting fact is that OS were not originally conceived for the latter purposes; their versatility of application was noticed during OSKAR's development. In the next sections, we will look at the way LILOG exploits this versatility, beginning with an overview of its representational medium.

4.3   The Knowledge Representation Language L_{LILOG}

The formal devices used in the LILOG project for representation and inferencing are the language L_{LILOG} and its "inference engine". L_{LILOG} is a consolidation of many standard features of contemporary KR languages, and its syntax and semantics are more or less standard as well. Thus the reader who is familiar with these standards might consider skipping right ahead to the OS application shown in sections 4.4 – 4.7. But the demands of rigor do not allow us to show an application of a language without saying anything about its syntax and formal interpretation. Our presentation will be limited to the fragment of L_{LILOG} that is actually applied in the next section, and the semantic interpretation we will consider is quite a bit simpler than the formal specification calls for.[30] The syntax assumed here for L_{LILOG} is implemented in the LEU/2 prototype; its semantics is based on the specification in Pletat/von Luck (1989). No prior knowledge of KR languages is assumed, but the reader should be familiar with the set-theoretic notation used to describe semantic interpretations.

L_{LILOG} can be thought of as a descendant of the KL-ONE family of languages (see Brachman/Schmolze 1985), Feature Logic (Smolka 1988), and many-sorted first-order predicate logic. As a KL-ONE descendant, L_{LILOG} has the set-theoretic tools needed to classify entities in a hierarchical structure. L_{LILOG} is thus a modern manifestation of the early semantic nets, organizing the world into a potentially rich taxonomy that is structured by a subsumption relation. By using symbols called **roles**, it is also possible to define and describe the properties of relations that hold between entities in the taxonomy. While conventional KL-ONE languages are restricted to descriptions of arbitrary binary relations, L_{LILOG} contains symbols called **features** that are interpreted as unary functions — hence the relationship to Feature Logic.

The notion of "meaning" for an L_{LILOG} representation is established by an open-world model-theoretic semantics. Stated briefly, semantic interpretations for L_{LILOG} are defined by specifying a **universe**, the set of entities that the representation can "be about", and an interpretation

---

[30]   For a more complete account of L_{LILOG}, the reader is referred to Pletat/von Luck (1989); for details on the inference engine and its proof strategies, see Bollinger et al. (1990).

function that maps L_{LILOG} expressions to appropriate components of the universe (this will be elaborated on below). The formal semantics makes it possible to verify the consistency of a representation and the validity of inferences, as well as to investigate formal properties of the language (such as its decision properties and computational complexity).

The classes of entities defined in an L_{LILOG} taxonomy are called **sorts**, and the language can be seen as a realization of order-sorted predicate logic (in which sortal restrictions on the application of a predicate are defined explicitly).[31] While classical order-sorted logic only allows for a set of sort names, L_{LILOG} provides set-theoretic operators, roles, and feature structures for the formation of arbitrarily complex **sort expressions**. Like sort names, sort expressions are interpreted as subsets of the universe, and hence induce an even richer structure in the universe than that induced by the ordering relation on sorts. This makes L_{LILOG} a powerful tool for describing the organization of the world to be modelled.

For the purposes of inferencing, the syntax of L_{LILOG} provides for quantified formulas (rules or facts) called **axioms**. Some of these axioms may be **default rules**, which specify assumptions that can be made in the absence of evidence to the contrary, but may be retracted if a contradiction is detected later. The LILOG system is equipped with an inference engine, an enhanced theorem prover that attempts to prove goals based on the axioms and sort hierarchy in the L_{LILOG} knowledge base. One component of the inference engine is a truth maintenance system (TMS), which keeps track of default assumptions and derived facts that depend on them. The TMS is responsible for revising a knowledge base when necessary in order to maintain its consistency.

4.3.1 Sorts and Sort Expressions

To begin our exposition on L_{LILOG} applications, let us first establish a shorthand for illustrating the way semantic models are specified for L_{LILOG} syntax. We will take an oversimplified approach here by assuming that a semantics for L_{LILOG} consists of only two components: a universe or domain of interpretation $\mathcal{D}$ (the set of entities that the representation can

---

31   Order-sorted predicate logic is attributed to Oberschelp (1962).

"be about"), and an interpretation function $[\![\cdot]\!]$ that maps L_{LILOG} expressions to subsets of, elements of, or relations on $\mathcal{D}$ and satisfies certain constraints, depending on the kind of expression being interpreted.

With this in mind, let us now consider declarations of sorts, atoms, features, and roles in L_{LILOG}. There are two "built-in" sort names, TOP and INT, which are assumed in any L_{LILOG} application. These are meant to correspond to the set of all entities and the set of integers, respectively (formally, $[\![\text{TOP}]\!] = \mathcal{D}$ and $[\![\text{INT}]\!] = \mathcal{Z}$, where $\mathcal{Z}$ is the set of integers); the numerals are assumed to be atoms belonging to the sort INT. User-defined sort names, as well as the atoms, features, and roles defined for them, are declared in a **sort hierarchy**, which simultaneously organizes the structure of sorts by means of a partial order. The sort hierarchy in L_{LILOG} corresponds to the TBox of a KL-ONE language ('T' for terminology). Suppose that we want to define subsorts of `object` called `artifact` and `natural_kind`; one subsort of `natural_kind` will be `human`, which is further subdivided into `man` and `woman`. We will let every human have an age, which is an integer, and there will be a relation "married" that holds between human beings. Finally, let's say that there are exactly four kinds of substances in the world, namely copper, wood, plastic and glass, and assume that every artifact consists of exactly one substance, and that every human being has made exactly one artifact. This can be described by the statements in a sort hierarchy shown in (84).[32]

Recall that sorts are interpreted in the formal semantics as subsets of the universe. That is, $[\![s]\!] \subseteq \mathcal{D}$ holds for any sort s. The built-in ordering relation < on sorts imposes further structural constraints on the sets they denote. In example (84), every interpretation of the sorts `human`, `man`, and `woman` must satisfy the requirements $[\![\text{man}]\!] \subseteq [\![\text{human}]\!]$ and $[\![\text{woman}]\!] \subseteq [\![\text{human}]\!]$ (here and in the following, all of the constraints shown for $[\![\cdot]\!]$ will hold for any model).

---

[32] The formal interpretation of "substance" in (84) seems quite unintuitive, since "copper", "water", and so on are interpreted as "objects" in the world, although they are really natural kinds. This would certainly be inadequate as a linguistic analysis; but we should bear in mind that a "semantic interpretation" in LILOG is simply a device that makes its formal properties precise, and need not be ascribed any more significance than that (this point will come up again in the next section).

```
(84)        sort substance         <    top;
              atoms copper, wood, plastic, glass.

            sort object            <    top.

            sort natural_kind      <    object.

            sort human             <    natural_kind;
              features   age        : int,
                         maker_of : artifact,
              roles      married :: human.

            sort man               <    human.

            sort woman             <    human.

            sort artifact          <    object;
              features   made_of : substance.
```

The relation that holds between two sorts s and s' when, in every interpretation, the set denoted by s contains the set denoted by s' is called **subsumption**; we say that s subsumes s' (in our example, human subsumes both man and woman). Subsumption is one of the most important pieces of information computed in a KR system, since it models inheritance and allows for inferences that are conditional on sort membership; in our example, it is easy to imagine assumptions that pertain only to women or only to men, and still others that are valid for human beings in general.

Features and roles are interpreted in the obvious way as unary functions and binary relations, respectively. In our example, the role married denotes a relation on the set denoted by human, and the feature age denotes a function mapping humans to integers; i.e., $[\![\mathrm{married}]\!] \subseteq [\![\mathrm{human}]\!] \times [\![\mathrm{human}]\!]$ and $[\![\mathrm{age}]\!] \in \mathbb{Z}^{[\![\mathrm{human}]\!]}$.[33] By restricting its features and roles to the sorts for which they are defined, L$_{\text{LILOG}}$ generalizes the techniques used in KL-ONE and Feature Logic, where roles and features are implictly defined for the top sort only.

The real expressive power of L$_{\text{LILOG}}$ comes to light when we combine sorts, features, roles, and atoms to form arbitrarily complex **sort expressions**. Like simple sort names, sort expressions denote subsets of the domain of interpretation, and two sort expressions stand in the subsumption relation if the set denoted by one is contained in the set denoted

---

[33]   The notation B^A stands for the set of all functions f given by $f: A \to B$.

by the other in every interpretation. The interpretation of a sort expression is computed simply by composing the interpretations of its constituents in a certain way. The simplest kind of sort expression is formed by a collection of atoms within the symbols '{', '}', which is interpreted as the set containing the interpretations of the atoms in the collection:

(85) $[\![\{a_1, \ldots, a_n\}]\!] = \{[\![a_1]\!], \ldots, [\![a_n]\!]\}$

A special shorthand for this kind of sort expression is used to define intervals of integers: the expression [0..4] denotes the interval from 0 to 4 (and is thus equivalent to the expression {0, 1, 2, 3, 4}).

More complex sort expressions can be formed by the set-theoretic operators and, or, and not, which are interpreted as forming the intersection, union, and complement (w.r.t $\mathcal{D}$), respectively, of the interpretations of their operands. We can continue our example with a redefinition of the sort man, by taking the sort woman as elementary and stating that man denotes that subset of the human beings that contains no women. Besides articulating a perhaps more feminist point of view, this definition expresses the fact that the sets of men and of women are disjoint.

(86)   sort man   =   and (human, not (woman)).

$[\![man]\!] = [\![human]\!] \cap \overline{[\![woman]\!]}$ $(= [\![human]\!] \setminus [\![woman]\!])$

One of the most useful techniques in LLILOG is the use of sort expressions that denote sets for which the range of a certain feature is constrained to a certain sort. A feature name f followed by a ':' and a sort expression se yields a new sort expression denoting the set of all entities whose image with respect to $[\![f]\!]$ lies in the set $[\![se]\!]$; i.e., $[\![f : se]\!] = \{x \in dom([\![f]\!]) \mid [\![f]\!](x) \in [\![se]\!]\}$, where $dom(f)$ is the domain of the function f.[34] The reader can confirm that the sort expression thus formed is implicitly subsumed by the sort for which the feature is declared. For

---

34   A similar technique is used in LLILOG to restrict the domain of roles, which we would use in our example to stipulate that men can only be married to women and women can only be married to men. But since roles are not used in the implementation of object schemata presented in this paper, we will not devote any further attention to them.

example, the sort expression in (87) below, which denotes the set of all entities whose age lies between 13 and 19, is a subsort of human (since the feature age was defined for human).

(87)   age : [13..19]

Note that the constraint given for the feature can be an arbitrarily complex sort expression, making it possible to define complex new sorts in terms of other sorts. Note also that if the sort expression se restricts the range of a feature f to a singleton set {a}, then the function $[\![f]\!]$ applied to any element of $[\![se]\!]$ must yield the value $[\![a]\!]$. We can make use of these two facts in our example by defining a sort teenager, which denotes the set of human beings aged between 13 and 19, and a sort furniture, denoting the set of artifacts made of wood:

(88)   sort teenager   =   and (human, age : [13..19]).

$$[\![teenager]\!] = [\![human]\!] \cap \{x \in dom([\![age]\!]) \mid [\![age]\!](x) \in [13, 19]\}$$
$$= \{x \in [\![human]\!] \mid [\![age]\!](x) \in [13, 19]\}$$

sort furniture =   and (artifact, made_of : {wood}).

$$[\![furniture]\!] \quad = \{x \in [\![artifact]\!] \mid [\![made\_of]\!](x) \in [\![\{wood\}]\!]\}$$
$$= \{x \in [\![artifact]\!] \mid [\![made\_of]\!](x) = [\![wood]\!]\}$$

The reader will notice that the syntax used in (88), where a supersort (human or artifact) is combined by the operator and with a feature constraint, is semantically redundant, since the feature constraint is implicitly subsumed by the supersort in both cases. The purpose is to aid the knowledge engineer by making the subsumption relation explicit. Defining subsorts in terms of constraints on the range of a feature is one of the most frequently used techniques in structuring a sort hierarchy, and it helps to be able to identify the supersort immediately.

The last type of sort expression to be presented here involves **feature paths**, a notion adopted from Feature Logic. A feature path is a list of feature names enclosed in the symbols '<', '>', corresponding to the iteration of the functions denoted by the features in the path. The features are listed in reverse order of their application, and the domain of each feature is required to lie in the range of its predecessor (the domain of the entire feature path is equal to the domain of its first feature, and its range equals the range of its last feature). The interpretation of a feature path can be thought of as follows (where ∘ is the symbol for the composition of functions):

(89) $[\![<f_1 \ldots f_n>]\!] = [\![f_n]\!] \circ \ldots \circ [\![f_1]\!]$

Thus feature paths can form structures that are as rich and complex as the sort hierarchies in which their features are defined. Feature paths are used in sort expressions to specify constraints on their range, just as we have done with simple features. To continue our example, suppose we want to define a sort `carpenter` to describe people who have made some furniture. We now have two ways of doing this, one of which is to take the subsort of `human` for which the feature `maker_of` is restricted to the sort `furniture` defined in (88) above. The other option is to use a feature path to state explicitly that the artifact denoted by the feature `maker_of` must be such that its value for `made_of` must be equal to `wood`. Hence we have the following equivalent definitions:

(90) `sort carpenter  =    and (human, maker_of : furniture).`

   `sort carpenter  =    and (human,`
   `                         <maker_of made_of> : {wood}).`

   $[\![\text{carpenter}]\!] = \{x \in [\![\text{human}]\!] \mid$
   $\qquad\qquad [\![\text{made\_of}]\!]([\![\text{maker\_of}]\!](x)) = [\![\text{wood}]\!]\}$

And with that we conclude our survey of the sort expressions of L$_{\text{LILOG}}$ used in this article. The sort description language with its complex feature structures will be applied in the following sections to define object schemata for natural sorts of objects, thus re-implementing in L$_{\text{LILOG}}$ the data structures shown for OSKAR in the foregoing report. But before we go on to the details, we must consider some of the other devices of L$_{\text{LILOG}}$ that we will make use of. These are necessary for writing rules that will duplicate the procedural aspects of OSKAR, and in particular for representing the contexts and contextual transitions of a natural-language text.

4.3.2 Referential Objects and Sortal Restrictions

Clearly, any representational formalism for knowledge extracted from texts requires special symbols that represent the mentioned objects: in L_LILOG these are called **referential objects**, or RefOs (see Habel 1986). RefOs are attached to sort expressions, and they are interpreted as elements of the set denoted by the sort to which they are assigned (thus the relationship between sorts and RefOs corresponds to the type-token distinction). Reference objects may be explicitly declared in a knowledge base, as in the declaration in (91) of the RefO r1 representing a female carpenter.

(91)   refo r1 : and (woman, carpenter).

But in many cases, RefOs will be generated automatically in the semantic analysis of a text in order to represent the denotation of a noun phrase. The sort assumed for a generated RefO is lexically determined in many cases, but may also be determined in part by the linguistic context in which the noun phrase occurs. In the applications we are interested in, RefOs will be generated for the physical objects mentioned in a text, and their sorts are determined lexically — "tower", "brick", and almost all of the other object concepts mentioned in the report name natural subsorts that can be anticipated in a sort hierarchy. RefOs are terms in L_LILOG, meaning that they can appear as arguments of functions or predicates or as the values of functions. In the representations shown below, we will assume that semantic analysis has already resolved noun phrase denotation in that a RefO has been selected for each referent.

Rules written in L_LILOG may make use of feature and role symbols as symbols for unary functions and binary predicates, respectively. The arguments of these expressions, as well as values returned by functions that correspond to features, are subject to the sortal restrictions established for them in the sort hierarchy. Specifically, if f is a feature symbol and r is a role symbol, where f denotes the function $f \in B^A$ and r denotes the relation $r \subseteq C \times D$, then the L_LILOG formulas f(a) = b and r(c,d) are **sortally correct** only if $[\![a]\!] \in A$, $[\![b]\!] \in B$, $[\![c]\!] \in C$ and $[\![d]\!] \in D$. In other words, the sorts assigned to the arguments and functional values in these expressions must be subsumed by the sorts defined for those positions. The restriction to sortally correct formulas exploits order-sorted logic by excluding propositions that are thought to be incoherent. In our example, it will not be possible to state that two artifacts are married to each other or that some human being made another human being because of the sortal restrictions placed on the respective roles and features.

In addition to features and roles, other kinds of functions and predicates may be defined and used in L$_{\text{LILOG}}$ rules. These are also subject to the sortal restrictions established by their declarations, and the conditions for their sortal correctness is a straightforward extension of the conditions given above for features and roles. We can further expand our example by adding a function `invented`, which maps pairs of humans and integers to artifacts, and a predicate `happy_family`, which relates women, men and artifacts.

```
(92) function invented (person:human, age:int) -> artifact.
     predicate happy_family (wife:woman, husband:man,
                                          family_car:artifact).
```

The important points to notice here are that user-defined functions and predicates have no restrictions as to their number of argument places, and that the arguments have "names", so that the order of arguments within the parentheses is irrelevant.

4.3.3   Rules and Facts

The last piece of L$_{\text{LILOG}}$ syntax to be presented here are rules and facts, collectively called axioms. L$_{\text{LILOG}}$ axioms are closed, quantified formulas in predicate logic with equality, employing the usual connectives `and`, `or`, `not`, `->`, `<->`, as well as `forall` and `exists` for the universal and existential quantifiers, respectively. Quantification in L$_{\text{LILOG}}$ adopts the method of order-sorted predicate logic in that it places sortal restrictions on its quantified variables: a variable of a particular sort `s` can only be instantiated by terms whose sort is subsumed by `s`. This is, in effect, a mechanism of user-defined rule selection for the theorem proving operation, since an axiom will not be taken in consideration in the proof of a goal unless its sortal restrictions are satisfied.

The following example of an L$_{\text{LILOG}}$ axiom guarantees the symmetry of the `married` relation:

```
(93)      axiom married_is_symmetric
             forall X,Y : human;
             married( X, Y )
             <->
             married( Y, X ).
```

As mentioned above, it is possible to write rules in L$_{LILOG}$ that support default assumptions to be made in the absence of evidence that contradicts them, allowing the inference engine to reason with incomplete knowledge. Just how to formalize defaults (a form of non-monotonic reasoning) is a matter of considerable interest in current AI research, and accordingly a wide variety of techniques with very different properties can be found in the literature.[35] L$_{LILOG}$ takes a novel approach in that it combines the default concept with the structure of the sort hierarchy, by taking defaults as generalized quantifiers over sorts. An axiom introduced by the quantification `default x : s` holds for most entities belonging to the sort s (where "most" can be defined as "more than half" or in some other appropriate way).

Thus a default assumption is interpreted in L$_{LILOG}$ as a statement that a certain proposition P holds for the majority of members of a sort s, and we can assume for any object x in [[s]] that it does indeed hold. Should we discover later that P does not hold for x after all, then we assume that it must have been one of the few exceptions and retract the assumption.[36] L$_{LILOG}$ defaults are illustrated in the final example, an axiom stating that most women are carpenters:

```
(94) axiom most_women_are_carpenters
          default W : woman;
          made_of(maker_of(W)) = wood.
```

And with that, our survey of the syntax and semantics of L$_{LILOG}$ to be applied in the representation of object schemata is complete.

---

35   Cf. Doyle (1983) and deKleer (1986), to name just two prominent examples.

36   There is quite a bit more to be said about non-monotonic reasoning in L$_{LILOG}$ (the complete, formal treatment is in Lorenz (1990)). — There are actually two kinds of default quantifiers `o_default` and `p_default`, denoting "optimistic" and "pessimistic" defaults, respectively. An optimistic default is thought to be more likely to hold, so that a consistency check can be deferred, whereas a consistency check for a pessimistic default is carried out immediately. But we will ignore this distinction and other details, just using `default` in the following.

4.4   Dimensional Designation and Positional Variation in LILOG

The integration of Lang's theory of dimensional designation and positional variation into the LILOG system proceeds in two steps:

(I) The structures developed in OSKAR must be re-implemented in L$_{\text{LILOG}}$; specifically, this means that the classifying elements of the language shown in 4.3.1 above are used to define object schemata, corresponding to the declarative part of OSKAR shown in 3.2 (see examples (51) – (55)). Likewise, we write rules of the kind presented in 4.3.3 to realize the procedures that operate on OS; their counterparts in OSKAR are shown in section 3.3. The technical details of the two implementations are rather different due to the differences between the languages, but essentially it is a straightforward matter of translating one notation into another. This is the main advantage of having a completed prototype.

(II) As mentioned above, the integration into LILOG must account for a number of issues left open by OSKAR, which we can now describe more precisely:

(a) The OS in OSKAR were defined for object concepts, not for individual objects in the world. In LILOG, we are interested in representing properties of objects mentioned in a text, and we might even have several instances of the same kind of object in a text with different OS due to different position properties. Technically speaking, we must take care of **inheritance** mechanisms that regulate the relationship between generic OS defined for object sorts and specified OS assigned to individual RefOs.

(b) Related to (a), the second requirement is a treatment of **context** and **context change**. OSKAR demonstrated the context dependency of dimensional expressions by modelling the various position properties of objects (*standing, lying, upside down*, etc.), but without representing contexts explicitly. In LILOG, we must work out what it means to say that an object has different position properties (and hence different OS) over time.

(c) The **Semantic Form** of dimensional terms shown in (21) and (23) above includes a scalar function QUANT, which yields a scalar value (a **degree**) for the designated object axis. The degree value is used in turn to represent information from a measurement phrase, comparative construction, etc. Using the explicit representation of object axes in OS, we can add the degree concept to the representation and define the QUANT function precisely.

In the remainder of this chapter, we will assume that semantic analysis of a text processes a dimensional term and resolves the reference of the object noun by selecting a RefO of the sort object, which instantiates the dimensional term's Semantic Form (coded in an appropriate way as an L$_{LILOG}$ predicate). Thus we can concentrate on the LILOG realization of the OS and the evaluation procedure demonstrated in OSKAR. First we will look at the integration of OS into the sort hierarchy, followed by the context-dependent assignment of OS. Finally, we will give a definition of the QUANT function in the form of an L$_{LILOG}$ axiom.

4.5   OS and Object Ontology in L$_{LILOG}$

Object schemata categorize objects into classes with respect to their gestalt and position properties, and both kinds of properties are represented uniformly in an OS. Essentially, the same is true in L$_{LILOG}$, but there is a distinction to be made as to where the two kinds of properties "come from". Gestalt properties and position properties emerging from intrinsic orientation and/or perspectivization of objects (cf. 2.2.3 and Fig. 8) are "object constitutive" and hence essential to our ontological knowledge of objects. They are invariable for all of the instances of a given sort. Among these are canonical position properties (see (30)(b) and (32)(a) above), which are assumed to hold for each object in a sort unless we have explicit information to the contrary (thus we assume the upright position of a tree or tower unless told otherwise). In contrast, "contextually induced" position properties of an object are determined by projections onto axes of the surrounding space in specific situations. As shown by the *breites Brett* example in (18), they vary as the object's position in space varies.

For the LILOG ontology, this means that object constitutive properties are encoded as primary entries of OS in the sort hierarchy, and these will never be altered. Contextually induced position properties of an object, which are not determined by its sort alone, are accounted for by specification rules applying to RefOs. Therefore, we use complex feature structures in the LILOG sort hierarchy to define OS that are assumed by default to hold for the elements of the various object sorts. In a second step, the assignment of the pertinent OS to an individual object in a specific context is realized by means of a default rule and a temporally-indexed L$_{LILOG}$ function (see section 4.6).

We begin by defining DAPs and DAVs in L$_{LILOG}$. All of the "theoretical entities" (such as OS) will belong to the sort SpatialConcept, an extremely general and unspecified sort that merely serves to keep technical notions of spatial knowledge separate from everything else in the sort hierarchy.[37] The OS shown here will be simpler than those shown in OSKAR in that the endpoints of object axes are not explicitly represented; this allows us to represent DAPs and DAVs simply as atoms collected in a subsort of SpatialConcept called DimDesignation (cf. the beginning of 3.2).

(95)   sort DimDesignation < SpatialConcept;
            atoms   max, vert, sub, dist, obs, across, imax,
                     ivert, iobs, d_sub, d_dist, diam, flach,
                     empty.

Having DAVs and DAPs in the same sort is a technical expedient (it facilitates unification); but the distinction established in sections 2.2, 3.2 and 4.2 remains valid. It is up to the knowledge engineer setting up the sort hierarchy to see to it that DAPs and DAVs are not confused.

The L$_{LILOG}$ sort Object has a feature default_schema, which is of the sort Objectschema. Thus a portion of our sort declaration for Object is:[38]

(96)   sort Object < SpatialEntity;
            features default_schema : Objectschema,
                  . . . .

---

[37]   The formal semantic interpretation of SpatialConcept and its subsorts seems rather odd, since things like object schemata and their components are interpreted as entities in the universe. Again, we should bear in mind that the formal interpretations are merely technical devices and do not imply that objects like OS are objects in the "real" world (cf. note 32 above).

[38]   The variations in OS mentioned in 2.3.1, as a means of treating **proportional variation** within an object class, can be accommodated in this scheme if we take disjunctions as constraints on the feature default_schema in the sort hierarchy; i.e a list of possible alternative OS can be defined for a natural subsort of objects such as "building".

The sort `Objectschema` is also a subsort of `SpatialConcept` (the list of object sides and the 'nop' attribute are neglected here). The two features of the sort `Objectschema` specify a dimensionality value (an integer between 1 and 3) and a list of entities of the sort `Section` (to be explained below).[39]

```
(97)      sort Objectschema < SpatialConcept,
            features      dimensions  : [1..3],
                          sections    : List_of_Sections.
```

The `sections` feature of an OS in LILOG corresponds to the OSKAR attribute of the same name in (49) above. Objects of the sort `Section` are also similar to the corresponding OSKAR attribute, shown here without the explicit representation of boundedness and endpoints, but with a new feature `degree` that associates each object axis with a scalar value:

```
(98)      sort Section < SpatialConcept;
            features      number_of_dims  : [1..3],
                          davs            : List_of_Davs,
                          degree          : SpatialDegrees.
```

In the LILOG system, the order of the DAVs in the "list of DAVs" feature is the opposite of that in OSKAR's `assignment` attribute. This is for technical reasons; whereas OSKAR accesses the last element of a section's assignment, it is more efficient to access the head of a list in the LILOG system. Seen as a data structure, the value of the `davs` feature is used as a stack, where the head of the list corresponds to the top of the stack, and the specification and de-specification operations correspond to push and pop, respectively.

In the sort hierarchy, the feature `davs` is assigned a list of the primary entries of an OS reflecting gestalt properties and its fixed or canonical position properties as discussed at the beginning of this section. As in OSKAR, contextually induced DAVs may be appended to the list in the course of processing a text; but this happens without affecting the OS defined in the sort hierarchy (see 4.6). The feature `number_of_dims`, like

---

[39] A list in L$_{\text{LILOG}}$ is inductively defined as in Prolog; a list is either a special object called the "empty list" (represented in L$_{\text{LILOG}}$ with the constant `nil`), or it consists of a feature `head`, which can be of any sort, and a feature `rest`, which is another list. But note that there are no built-in list processing services in L$_{\text{LILOG}}$.

OSKAR's `axes` attribute, indirectly specifies the axis' integratedness as a dimensionality value. The use of the feature `degree` will become clear when the realization of the QUANT function is presented in 4.7.

Given these sort definitions, we can define the OS of an object sort by assigning appropriate values to feature paths in its sort declaration. We are now in a position to retrace the history of object schemata through all three stages: theory, prototype, and integration. Taking the OS of "valley", "tree" and "pole" as examples (objects with fixed, canonical and unspecified orientation, respectively), we see how conceptually constant OS are encoded in various task-specific notations.

(99)   "valley"   "tree"   "pole"
        ‹ a   b   c ›   ‹ a   (b   c) ›   ‹ a   (b   c) ›
        max   ø   vert   max   sub   max   sub
                  obs   vert

(100) "valley"

```
os([  dimensions([a,b,c]),
      sections([  section([  axes([a]),
                             boundedness(bounded),
                             endpoints([a1,a2]),
                             assignment([max(a1,a2)])]),
                  section([  axes([b]),
                             boundedness(bounded),
                             endpoints([b1,b2]),
                             assignment([empty(b1,b2)])])]),
                  section([  axes([c]),
                             boundedness(bounded),
                             endpoints([c1,c2]),
                             assignment([vert(c1,c2),obs(c2,c1)])])])]),
      nop('*'),
      sides([ s(a1,_,_),s(a2,_,_),s(b1,_,_),s(b2,_,_), s(c1,_,_),
              s(c2,_,_)]) ])
```

(101) "tree"

```
os([  dimensions([a,b,c]),
      sections([  section([  axes([a]),
                             boundedness(bounded),
                             endpoints([a1,a2]),
                             assignment([max(a1,a2),vert(a1,a2)])]),
                  section([  axes([b,c]),
                             boundedness(bounded),
                             endpoints([d1,d2]),
                             assignment([sub(d1,d2)])])]),
      nop('*'),
      sides([ s(a1,i_us,_), s(a2,i_os,_),s(d1,_,_),s(d2,_,_)]) ])
```

(102) "pole"

```
os([ dimensions([a,b,c]),
     sections([ section([ axes([a]),
                          boundedness(bounded),
                          endpoints([a1,a2]),
                          assignment([max(a1,a2)])]),
                section([ axes([b,c]),
                          boundedness(bounded),
                          endpoints([d1,d2]),
                          assignment([sub(d1,d2)])])]),
                nop('*'),
     sides([ s(a1,_,_), s(a2,_,_),s(d1,_,_),s(d2,_,_)]) ])
```

(103) sort valley < and (Object,
```
           default_schema :
                  and(dimensions : {3},
                      <sections head> :
                          and( number_of_dims : {1},
                               <davs head> : {max},
                               <davs rest> : {nil}),
                      <sections rest head> :
                          and( number_of_dims : {1},
                               <davs head> : {empty},
                               <davs rest> : {nil}),
                      <sections rest rest head> :
                          and( number_of_dims : {1},
                               <davs head> : {obs},
                               <davs rest head> : {vert},
                               <davs rest rest> : {nil}),
                      <sections rest rest rest> : {nil})).
```

(104) sort tree < and (Object,
```
           default_schema :
                  and(dimensions : {3},
                      <sections head> :
                          and( number_of_dims : {1},
                               <davs head> : {vert},
                               <davs rest head> : {max},
                               <davs rest rest> : {nil}),
                      <sections rest head> :
                          and( number_of_dims : {2},
                               <davs head> : {sub},
                               <davs rest> : {nil}),
                      <sections rest rest> : {nil})).
```

(105) sort pole < and (Object,
```
           default_schema :
                  and(dimensions : {3},
                      <sections head> :
                          and( number_of_dims : {1},
                               <davs head> : {max},
                               <davs rest> : {nil}),
                      <sections rest head> :
                          and( number_of_dims : {2},
                               <davs head> : {sub},
                               <davs rest> : {nil}),
                      <sections rest rest> : {nil})).
```

4.6   Inheritance and Context Dependent Assignment of OS to RefOs

The sort declarations in (103) – (105) define context invariant gestalt properties and intrinsic position properties of certain kinds of objects. Now we must go on to the context-dependent assignment of OS in a representation, which is closely related to the assignment of **positional properties and variations** to individual objects described in 3.3 above. When an object is introduced in discourse (i.e. when a RefO is generated for it), the OS determined by the object's sort is assumed by default, and hence it takes on the canonical positional properties defined there as well. For example, if a tree is mentioned in a text, it is assumed to be in upright position (thus that its specified OS contains entries for vertical orientation, as in (104)) unless we have explicit evidence to the contrary. If the object undergoes a change in its position (say the tree is felled), or if the assumption about its position is explicitly contradicted in the subsequent text, then based on the original OS, a new OS' which is appropriate to the new position is assigned to the RefO in question.

The only contextual parameter that is assumed here to be relevant in positional variation is time, since an object can have at most one position property at any moment. Its spatial location, for example, can be left out of consideration, because whether an object is *standing, lying, upside down,* etc. does not depend on how it is localized with respect to other objects. Thus to cope with the context dependence and default status of OS in LILOG, we will create RefOs of the sort Objectschema in L_{LILOG}, which are assigned to object RefOs by means of the temporally indexed L_{LILOG} function has-os. This function has the following arguments and sortal restrictions:

(106)   function has-os(Obj:Object, Temp:Interval)
                                              -> Objectschema.

When a RefO of the sort Object is introduced into the representation, the following default rule assigns it an OS that is identical with the default schema from its sort:

```
(107)    axiom default_object_schema
             forall OS:Objectschema, T:Interval;
             default O:Object;
             default_schema(O) = OS
             ->
             has-os( Obj:O, Temp:T ) = OS.
```

Modifications of that initial OS may i.a. be due to (a) positional specification (e.g. *the pole is 2m tall* entails the pole's upright position) or (b) positional change (e.g. *the tree has been felled* entails that the tree's canonical verticality and situational orientation are at variance). Both of these result in an OS' reflecting the object's new position, which in each case is created in the specification process by the procedural part. However, the different kinds of specification have differing consequences for the LILOG representation.

In case (a), positional specification, the default assumption according to (107) of the pole's object schema (shown in (105)) has been contradicted and must be retracted, meaning that the old OS is overwritten by the new OS'. But in case (b), positional change, the object has undergone a physical transition from one position to another, which is modelled by having the has-os function associate its RefO with OS' under a new temporal index.

In declaration (106), Interval is the sort of temporal intervals. These are the entities proposed for LILOG for the treatment of tense and aspect; they are created and structured by the component responsible for temporal knowledge (cf. Eberle 1988, 1989). In order to see how we arrive at a value for the argument Temp in (107), we must take a closer look at LILOG's treatment of the relevant verbs. We distinguish **static verbs of position** such as *stehen* and *liegen* (*stand, lie* ; cf. section 3.3.3) from their **causative** derivatives *stellen, legen* (*set upright, lay down*). In addition to specifying a local argument and tense and aspectual information, the meaning of each of these verbs encompasses a **mode of position** (for details see Maienborn 1990). In OSKAR, modes of position have been worked out precisely as the conditions given in 3.3.2 and 3.3.3 above. Recall that a mode of position involves characteristic relations between the object's axes and the Vertical and/or Observer axis of the surrounding space, and is manifested by the occurrence of vert and/or obs in the object's OS and by entries of its deictic and intrinsic side assignments.

For the static verbs of position as well as predicates such as *to be upside down* and *to be on edge*, the mode of position is realized as an evaluation of the matching conditions with the OS of the object in question, as shown in 3.3.3. Now it is clear that the OS reflecting a static position remains constant for a given object as long as the object retains that position. This means that the value of temporal index produced to model the tense/aspect of a static verb like *stehen* coincides with the value of the index Temp in an instance of the has-os function .

The causative verbs *stellen, legen* and the verbs of positional change *tilt* and *turn* from section 3.3.2. indicate a change of state, meaning that the interval T associated with the previous state is closed, and a new interval T' is created for the ensuing state. The temporal structures ascribed to the causative verbs of position in LILOG are similar to the event structures proposed in Moens & Steedman (1988), who assume characteristic **consequent states** for the state transitions denoted by event verbs. The verbs *legen* and *stellen*, for example, introduce consequent states appropriate for the static verbs *liegen* and *stehen*. Similarly, the verbs *tilt*, *turn*, and so on introduce consequent states that are characterized by the modified object schemata shown in section 3.3.3. The new temporal index T' created for the consequent state is taken up in the has-os function in order to assign an OS' to the object in question. Thus in LILOG, we combine the modification of OS accounting for positional variation as implemented in OSKAR with the treatment of temporal intervals that are needed to account for tense and aspect of verbs. The context dependent assignment of OS to objects in the LILOG system is a capability that is crucial in the transition from OSKAR to a text comprehension system.

4.7   Dimensional Designation and Scalar Functions

Now that we know how object schemata are defined for object sorts and attached to RefOs representing specific objects in specific contexts, we have the prerequisites for re-implementing the dimensional designation process and the Semantic Form of dimensional terms in LLILOG. As proclaimed in the heading of section 2.4, dimensional designation consists of mapping DAPs onto OS; within OSKAR, the **evaluation** of a DAP with respect to an OS has been worked out even more precisely: evaluation consists of either identifying or specifying a DAV in the OS so as to locate the designated object axis. Having added a temporal index in LILOG as a contextual parameter, we now make evaluation dependent on a temporal location as well; that is, a dimensional term will be evaluated with respect to the temporal information available from the sentence in which it occurs.

In LLILOG, a function `eval_DAP` is defined which is the counterpart to OSKAR's evaluation procedure in (56) above. This function returns the OS-section representing the axis designated by a given DAP; to determine its value, a set of LLILOG rules that carry out the identification and specification procedures is started. This process is essentially identical to that shown in 3.3.1; the only important difference is that OSKAR's "change and copy" operation is replaced by the mechanisms of default reasoning and context change explained in the previous section.

```
(108) function eval_DAP(DAP:DimDesignation, OS:Objectschema)
                                            -> Section.
```

The function `eval_DAP` is embedded in a definition of the QUANT function, which in turn is a constituent of the Semantic Form of dimensional terms as indicated in section 2.1.5. We assume a theory of dimensional expressions as **gradables**, a class including adjectives that characteristically allow measurement phrases and comparative constructions as in (109) – (111):

(109)   This tree is 10m in height.
(110)   This tree is higher than that tower.
(111)   The bookcase is wider than high.

We model the degree to which an object possesses the property denoted by the expression in question (the extent of object axes in the case of dimensional terms) by making assertions about theoretical objects called "degrees". Sentence (109) is treated by assigning a measurement value to a degree, while sentences (110) – (111) are accounted for by placing the degrees of height of the mentioned objects in an ordering relation.[40] The purpose of the feature `degree` of `Section` is to assign a unique degree to each object axis.

---

[40]   The theory of gradation underlying the Semantic Form shown here is given in Bierwisch (1989); another comprehensive theory of degree adjectives is worked out in von Stechow (1984), which includes a survey and critique of various rival theories.

Thus to realize the QUANT function in L<small>LILOG</small>, we execute the evaluation procedure for a given DAP to pick out an OS-section and return the degree object assigned to that section. The declaration of QUANT now including a temporal index is as follows:

(112)   ```
function QUANT(DAP:DimDesignation, Obj:Object,
                        Temp:Interval) -> SpatialDegrees.
```

The intended meaning of QUANT is captured by combining the `has-os` and `eval_DAP` functions in the following axiom:

(113)     ```
axiom quant_definition
        forall X:Object, DIM:DimDesignation, T:Interval,
                D:Degree, S:Section;
        QUANT (DIM, X, T) = D
        <->
        has-os(X, T) = OS
        and
        eval_DAP(DIM, OS) = S
        and
        degree(S) = D.
```

This means that the value assigned to an object extent for a DAP DIM at T is equal to the value of the feature `degree` for the OS section returned by `eval_DAP`.

To come around to the end of our sketch of the QUANT function, we note that by using degrees to fix information about object extents, we can account for the inferences involving dimensional terms that have been mentioned so often. Taking up the familiar example (20) treated in 2.4.2 and 3.5.4, we interpret the statement that a pole is *5m high* in a certain context as saying that the scale value associated with its vertically oriented axis is assigned the measurement *5m*. This measurement information is retained when the pole's position is changed in such a way that the OS-section containing the DAV `vert` is de-specified (e.g. when the pole is laid down on the ground), so that the dimensional term *length* will correctly identify the value *5m* in this case. Along the same lines, relations between object axes expressed in comparatives (e.g. (110) – (111)) can now be retained over context changes induced by positional manipulation.

Before the curtain closes, let's recollect the performances of the various characters in our play of three acts. The final chapter has portrayed a knowledge engine which has benefitted greatly from having a sophisticated prototype at its disposal. This comes from the rigor that the Prolog program gains by taking serious linguistics seriously. All in all, the project confirms our view that linguistic theorizing about spatial knowledge is good for keeping the gray cells going, and more.

OSKAR entered the stage to bring linguists and AI researchers together. As we draw the curtain, the closing lines delivered by OSKAR are these:

Don't just talk about co-operation – do it!

Literature

Bierwisch, M. (1967): Some semantic universals of German adjectivals. *Foundations of Language* 3. 1 - 36

Bierwisch, M. (1988): On the Grammar of Local Prepositions. In: M. Bierwisch, W. Motsch, I. Zimmermann (eds.) Syntax, Semantik und Lexikon. 1-65. Berlin: Akademie-Verlag

Bierwisch, M. (1989): The Semantics of Gradation. In: M. Bierwisch, E. Lang (eds.)(1989). 71 - 261

Bierwisch, M., Lang, E. (eds.)(1987): Grammatische und konzeptuelle Aspekte von Dimensionsadjektiven. Berlin: Akademie-Verlag

Bierwisch, M., Lang, E. (eds.)(1989): Dimensional Adjectives: Grammatical Structure and Conceptual Interpretation. Berlin-Heidelberg-New York: Springer-Verlag

Bierwisch, M., Lang. E. (1987a): Etwas länger - viel tiefer - immer weiter. Epilog zum Dimensionsadjektiveprojekt. In: M. Bierwisch, E. Lang (eds.)(1987), pp. 649 - 699.

Bierwisch, M., Lang. E. (1989a): Somewhat Longer - Much Deeper - Further and Further. Epilogue to the Dimension Adjective Project. In: M. Bierwisch, E. Lang (eds.) (1989), pp. 471-514

Blutner, R. (in press): The Ontology of Spatial Concepts: The Fallacy of the so-called M - Principle. In: Proceedings of the International Theodor-Fechner-Symposium. Leipzig: S. Hirzel Verlag

Bollinger, T., Hedtstück, U., and Pletat, U. (1990): The LILOG Inference Engine. In: Geurts (ed.).

Bosch, P., Rollinger, C.R., Studer, R. (eds.) (1991): Text Understanding in LILOG: Integrating Computational Linguistics and Artificial Intelligence. Berlin-Heidelberg-New York: Springer-Verlag

Brachman, R., Schmolze, J. (1985): An Overview of the KL-ONE Knowledge Representation System. *Cognitive Science* 9(2), 171 - 216

Carstensen, K.-U., Simmons, G. (1991): Why a hill can't be a valley: Representing Gestalt and Position Properties of Objects with Object Schemata. In: Bosch et al. (eds.).

Clark, H. H. (1973): Space, Time, Semantics, and the Child. In: T. E. Moore (ed.): Cognitive Development and the Acquisition of Language. pp. 28 - 63. New York: Academic Press

Clark, H. H., Clark, E.V. (1977): Psychology and Language. An Introduction to Psycholinguistics. New York: Harcourt and Brace

deKleer, J. (1986): An Assumption-Based Truth Maintenance System. *Artificial Intelligence* 28, 127-162

Doyle, J. (1983): The Ins and Outs of Reason Maintenance. Proceedings of IJCAI-83, Karlsruhe. pp. 349-351. Los Altos, CA: Morgan Kaufman

Eberle, K. (1988): Eine Prolog-Theorie für zeitliche Beziehungen zwischen Ereignissen. LILOG-Report 14. Stuttgart: IBM Deutschland GmbH

Eberle, K. (1989): Quantifikation, Plural, Ereignisse und ihre Argumente in einer mehr-sortigen Sprache der Prädikatenlogik erster Stufe. IWBS Report 67. Stuttgart: IBM Deutschland GmbH

Farah, M. J. (1988): Is Visual Imagery really Visual? Overlooked Evidence From Neuropsychology. *Psychological Review* 95 : 3, 307-317

Fodor, J. A. (1983): The Modularity of Mind. An Essay on Faculty Psychology. Cambridge, Mass.: MIT Press

Geurts, B. (ed.) (1990): Natural Language Understanding in LILOG: An Intermediate Overview. IWBS Report 137. IBM Deutschland GmbH

Habel, C. (1986): Prinzipien der Referentialität. Untersuchungen zur propositionalen Repräsentation von Wissen. Informatik Fachberichte 122. Berlin: Springer

Habel, C. (1988): Cognitive Linguistics: The Processing of Spatial Concepts. LILOG - Report 45. Stuttgart: IBM Deutschland GmbH

Habel, C. (1989): zwischen-Bericht. In: C. Habel et al. (eds.): Raumkonzepte in Verstehensprozessen. pp. 37-69. Tübingen: Niemeyer

Habel, C. (1990): Propositional and Depictorial Representations of Spatial Knowledge: The Case of path-concepts. In : R. Studer (ed.): Natural Language and Logic. Lecture Notes in Artificial Intelligence, vol. 459. pp. 94 - 117. Berlin-Heidelberg-New York: Springer-Verlag

Harris, P.L., Morris, J.E., Meerum Terwogt, M. (1986): The Early Acquisition of Spatial Adjectives: A Cross-Linguistic Study. *Journal of Child Language* 13, 335-352

Hayes, P. J. (1985): The Second Naive Physics Manifesto. In: J. R. Hobbs, R. C. Moore (eds.): Formal Theories of the Commonsense World. pp. 1 - 36. Norwood, N. J.: Ablex Publishing Corp.

Herskovits, A. (1986): Language and Spatial Cognition. An Interdisciplinary Study of the Prepositions in English. Cambridge: Cambridge University Press

Herskovits, A. (1988): Spatial Expressions and the Plasticity of Meaning. In: B. Rudzka-Ostyn (ed.): Topics in Cognitive Linguistics. pp. 403 - 427. Amsterdam-Philadelphia: Benjamins

Herweg, M.(1989): Ansätze zu einer semantischen Beschreibung topologischer Präpositionen. In: C. Habel et al. (eds.) Raumkonzepte in Verstehensprozessen. pp. 99 - 127. Tübingen: Niemeyer

Herzog, O. et al. (1986): LILOG – Linguistic and Logical Methods for the Computational Understanding of German. LILOG Report 1b. Stuttgart: IBM Deutschland GmbH

Hlebec, B. (1983): A Lexico-semantic Study of English One-Dimension Adjectives. Belgrade: *Anali filoloskog fakulteta* 15, 243 - 280

Hottenroth, P.-M. (1988) : Die Semantik lokaler Präpositionen. Ein prototypensemantisches Modell für die französische Präposition *dans* mit einer Analyse der Beziehungen zwischen der Präposition und den Objektbezeichnungen in den Präpositionalsyntagmen. Habilitationsschrift, Universität Konstanz

Jackendoff, R. (1983): Semantics and Cognition. Cambridge, Mass.: MIT Press

Jackendoff, R. (1990): Semantic Structures. Cambridge, Mass.: MIT Press

Kaufmann, I. (1989): Direktionale Präpositionen. In: C. Habel et al. (eds.) Raumkonzepte in Verstehensprozessen. pp. 128-149. Tübingen: Niemeyer

Klose, G., von Luck, K. (1990): Knowledge Engineering. In: Geurts (ed.)

Klose, G., von Luck, K. (1991): The Representation of Knowledge in LILOG. In: Bosch et al. (eds.)

Kosslyn, S. M. (1980): Image and Mind. Cambridge, Mass.: Harvard University Press

Lafrenz, P. G. (1983): Zu den semantischen Strukturen der Dimensions-Adjektive in der deutschen Gegenwartssprache. Göteborg: University Publishers

Lakoff, G. (1987): Women, Fire, and Dangerous Things. What Categories Reveal about the Mind. Chicago: University of Chicago Press

Lakoff, G. (1988): Cognitive Semantics. In: U. Eco et al. (eds): Meaning and Mental Representations. pp. 119-154. Bloomington: Indiana University Press

Lang, E. (1987): Semantik der Dimensionsauszeichnung räumlicher Objekte. In: M. Bierwisch, E. Lang (eds.)(1987). pp. 287 - 458

Lang, E. (1987b): Gestalt und Lage räumlicher Objekte: Semantische Struktur und kontextuelle Interpretation von Dimensionsadjektiven. In: J. Bayer (ed.): Grammatik und Kognition. Psycholinguistische Untersuchungen. pp. 163 - 191. Opladen: Westdeutscher Verlag

Lang, E. (1988): Objekt Schemata and Räumliche Konfigurationen. Papier zum DFG-Projekt "Räumliche Lokalisierung". Düsseldorf: Heinrich-Heine-Universität Düsseldorf

Lang, E. (1989a): The Semantics of Dimensional Designation of Spatial Objects. In: M. Bierwisch, E. Lang (eds.), pp. 263 - 417.

Lang, E. (1989b): Primärer Orientierungsraum und inhärentes Proportionsschema. In: C. Habel et al. (eds.) Raumkonzepte in Verstehensprozessen. pp. 150-173. Tübingen: Niemeyer

Lang, E. (1990a): Primary Perceptual Space and Inherent Proportion Schema. Journal of Semantics 7, 121 – 141

Lang, E. (1990b): A Two-Level Approach to Projective Prepositions. In: G. Rauh (ed.)

Lang, E., Carstensen, K.-U. (1989a): OSKAR - ein Prolog-Programm zur Modellierung der Struktur und Verarbeitung räumlichen Wissens. In: D. Metzing (ed.): GWAI '89. 13th German Workshop on Artificial Intelligence. pp. 234 - 243. Berlin-Heidelberg-New York: Springer-Verlag

Lang, E., Carstensen, K.-U. (1990): OSKAR – A Prolog Program for Modelling Dimensional Designation and Positional Variation of Objects in Space. IWBS Report 109. Stuttgart: IBM Deutschland GmbH

Langacker, R. W. (1987): Foundations of Cognitive Grammar. Vol. I. Theoretical Prerequisites. Stanford, CA: Stanford University Press

Lehrer, A. (1974): Semantic Fields and Lexical Structure. Amsterdam: North-Holland

Lorenz, S. (1990): Nicht-monotones Schließen mit Ordnungssortierten Defaults. IWBS Report 100. Stuttgart: IBM Deutschland GmbH

Lyons, J. (1977): Semantics. Vol.1, 2 .Cambridge: Cambridge University Press

Maienborn, C. (1990): Position und Bewegung: Zur Semantik lokaler Verben. IWBS Report 138. Stuttgart: IBM Deutschland GmbH

Marr, D. (1982): Vision. San Francisco, CA: Freeman

Miller, G. A., Johnson-Laird, P. N. (1976): Language and Perception. Cambridge: Cambridge University Press

Moens, M. / Steedman, M. (1988): Temporal Ontology and Temporal Reference. *Computational Linguistics* 4:2, 15-28

Oberschelp, A. (1962): Untersuchungen zur mehrsortigen Quantorenlogik. *Mathematische Annalen* 145, 297-333

Patel-Schneider, P. F. (1984): Small can be Beautiful in Knowledge Representation. Proc. IEEE Workshop on Principles of Knowledge-Based Systems, Denver. pp. 11-16. Los Alamitos, CA: IEEE Computer Society Press

Pinker, S. (1984): Visual Cognition: An Introduction. *Cognition* 18, 1-63

Pletat, U., von Luck, K. (1989): Knowledge Representation in LILOG. IWBS Report 90. Stuttgart: IBM Deutschland GmbH

Pribbenow, S. (1991): Phenomena of Localization. In: P. Bosch et al. (eds.)

Rauh, G. (1990)(ed.): Approaches to Prepositions. Tübingen: Gunter Narr Verlag

Rehkämper, K. (1988): Mentale Bilder - Analoge Repräsentationen. LILOG-Report 65. Stuttgart: IBM Deutschland GmbH

Schwarze, C. (1989): Das Lexikon der Raumbeschreibung im Französischen. Arbeitspapier Universität Konstanz

Smolka, G. (1988): A Feature Logic with Subsorts. LILOG Report 33. Stuttgart: IBM Deutschland GmbH

von Stechow, A. (1985): Comparing Semantic Theories of Comparison. *Journal of Semantics* 3, 1 - 77

Vandeloise, C. (1986): L'Espace en français. Sémantique des prépositions spatiales. Paris: Éditions du Seuil

Wenger, K. (1988): Syntax und Semantik von Dimensionsausdrücken. Magisterarbeit. Universität Tübingen.

Wunderlich, D. (1986): Raum und die Struktur des Lexikons. In: Bosshardt, H.- G. (ed.): Perspektiven auf Sprache. Interdisziplinäre Beiträge zum Gedenken an Hans Hörmann. pp. 212-231. Berlin: de Gruyter

Wunderlich, D., Herweg, M. (1990): Lokale und Direktionale. In: von Stechow, A., Wunderlich, D. (eds.): Handbuch der Semantik. Berlin: de Gruyter

List of Figures

Lecture Notes in Computer Science

This subseries of the Lecture Notes in Computer Science reports new developments in Artificial Intelligence research and teaching – quickly, informally and at a high level. The type of material considered for publication includes preliminary drafts of original papers and monographs, technical reports of high quality and broad interest, advanced level lectures, reports of meetings, provided they are of exceptional interest and focused on a single topic. The timeliness of a manuscript is more important than its form which may be unfinished or tentative. If possible, a subject index should be included. Publication of Lecture Notes is intended as a service to the international computer science community, in that a commercial publisher, Springer-Verlag, can offer a wide distribution of documents which would otherwise have a restricted readership. Once published and copyrighted, they can be referred to in the scientific literature.

Manuscripts

Manuscripts should be no less than 100 and preferably no more than 500 pages in length.

They are reproduced by a photographic process and therefore must be prepared with extreme care according to the instructions available from the publisher. Proceedings' editors and authors of monographs receive 75 free copies. Authors of contributions to proceedings are free to use the material in other publications upon notification to the publisher. The typescript is reduced slightly in size during reproduction; best results will not be obtained unless the text on any one page is kept within the overall limit of $18 \times 26,5$ cm ($7 \times 10\frac{1}{2}$ inches). On request, the publisher will supply special paper with the typing area outlined.

Manuscripts should be sent to Prof. J. Siekmann, Institut für Informatik, Universität Kaiserslautern, Postfach 30 49, D-6750 Kaiserslautern, FRG, or directly to Springer-Verlag Heidelberg.

Springer-Verlag, Heidelberger Platz 3, D-1000 Berlin 33
Springer-Verlag, Tiergartenstraße 17, D-6900 Heidelberg 1
Springer-Verlag, 175 Fifth Avenue, New York, NY 10010/USA
Springer-Verlag, 37-3, Hongo 3-chome, Bunkyo-ku, Tokyo 113, Japan

---

ISBN 3-540-53718-X
ISBN 0-387-53718-X